Foundations of Stage Makeup

Foundations of Stage Makeup is a comprehensive exploration into the creative world of stage makeup. Step-by-step makeup applications paired with textual content create an enriching experience for future performers and makeup artists. Students will learn relevant history, color theory, makeup sanitation processes, and the use of light and shadow to engage in discussions about the aspects of professional makeup. Those foundations are then paired with a semester's-worth of descriptive, engaging makeup applications. Old age makeup, blocking out eyebrows, gory burns, and creating fantastical creatures are just a few of the rewarding techniques found in *Foundations of Stage Makeup*. The book is complemented by an eResource page featuring makeup tutorials and an instructor's manual with example assignments and tips to teaching each chapter.

Daniel C Townsend has worked as a Wigmaster and makeup artist in the theatre industry for over a decade. With his Master of Fine Arts degree from the University of Cincinnati – College Conservatory of Music, he has taught collegiate stage makeup and wig making courses, toured internationally, and served as Wigmaster for both Colorado and Utah Shakespeare Festivals as well as for the regional theatre Cincinnati Playhouse in the Park.

Foundations of Stage Makeup

Daniel C Townsend

Routledge
Taylor & Francis Group

NEW YORK AND LONDON

First published 2019
by Routledge
52 Vanderbilt Avenue, New York, NY 10017

and by Routledge
2 Park Square, Milton Park, Abingdon, Oxon, OX14 4RN

Routledge is an imprint of the Taylor & Francis Group, an informa business

Library of Congress Cataloging-in-Publication Data
Names: Townsend, Daniel C., author.
Title: Foundations of stage makeup / Daniel C Townsend.
Description: New York, NY : Routledge, 2019. | Includes bibliographical
references.
Identifiers: LCCN 2018056356 (print) | LCCN 2018056768 (ebook) |
ISBN 9780429946790 (Adobe Reader) | ISBN 9780429946776 (Mobipocket
Unencrypted) | ISBN 9780429946783 (ePub3) | ISBN 9781138594876
(hardback : alk. paper) | ISBN 9781138595019 (pbk. : alk. paper) |
ISBN 9780429487729 (ebook)
Classification: LCC PN2068 (ebook) | LCC PN2068 .T674 2019 (print) |
DDC 792.02/7—dc23
LC record available at https://lccn.loc.gov/2018056356

ISBN: 978-1-138-59487-6 (hbk)
ISBN: 978-1-138-59501-9 (pbk)
ISBN: 978-0-429-48772-9 (ebk)

Typeset in Gill Sans
by Apex CoVantage, LLC

Visit the eResources: www.routledge.com/9781138595019

CONTENTS

PREFACE

Several years ago, I was invited to teach stage makeup at Northern Kentucky University. With a Master of Fine Art degree from the University of Cincinnati – College Conservatory of Music and my years of experience as a wigmaster and makeup artist, I felt more than prepared for the routine of teaching. My intent was to find a text from which I could build my course, a book that would allow the students to follow along outside of class. I wanted my class to be a balanced mix between knowledge-based learning – anatomy, colors, light, history – and real makeup application. My hope was to find a book that would aid me in this instruction and be a starting point for supportive material. The search led me to several well-known texts, but each one lacked current photographs or relevant class material. Often these texts included information not necessary for collegiate performers, or the information was outdated.

Through discussions with other university instructors – professionals who also taught stage makeup – I found several unfortunate truths. The instructors felt unsupported when it came to stage makeup textbooks. They described the available resources just as I had, dated and irrelevant. And to make matters worse, many instructors did not have intensive makeup training to teach the material effectively or with confidence.

As I built my syllabus and reworked it over the following years, my desire to help my colleagues never changed. It did not take me long to start working on this project, one that had been in development for three years. There were two factors that contributed to the writing of this book.

The first factor was my own students. Every Thursday I would demonstrate a makeup to the students, and each Tuesday they would be graded on the makeup. The expectation was that they practice at home. Many did, yet the practice was always inconsistent. Their notes taken in classes and pictures taken during demonstrations were not enough. I never found a useful textbook for class, so they had no guide to follow. *Foundations of Stage Makeup* is the book I could not find – a photographic record for students to practice outside of class and a resource to be used instead of scribbled notes. Performers would finally learn practical makeup applications which could benefit them in their careers; technicians would have a class providing a basis for their work in the industry.

The second factor was for teachers and instructors. There was one thing lacking when I talked with my colleagues: makeup experience. Formal stage makeup training is not common, only being found in university theatre departments, and often taught by individuals not confident in his or her ability to teach the subject. This

text seeks to empower instructors at beginning levels – high school and university – with tools and resources for consistent instruction. The corresponding video tutorials will make it easy for instructors to learn the applications for their own in-class demonstrations and teach them with confidence.

It has been a journey condensing my experience into this book and the online materials. If there is one thing teaching my own class has taught me, it is that nothing is permanent. What is relevant today will not be relevant tomorrow. My hope is that, by using this book, readers will gain the experience they need now, so they can continue to grow and learn in the future. This book has changed my life, and I hope it changes others as well.

ACKNOWLEDGMENTS

I would like to acknowledge the following individuals for their contribution to the creation of this book, the videos, and the online content. None of this would have been possible without their sacrifices: Jessica Townsend, editors Stacey Walker and Lucia Accorsi, proofreader Brandi Brooks, photographer Adam Zeek of Zeek Creative, and my video team Justin Eckstein and Aaron Allen. The models are D'Waughn and Anna Hazard, Gabriella Sam, Taylor Germany, Jenna Hawks, and Ming Wang. Thanks go also to my mentors Robert Haven and Kelly Yurko, and to God, in whom all things are possible.

INTRODUCTION

Have you ever seen a performance and been wowed by the makeup? Many performers take years to learn stage makeup application. In the most prestigious theatres, there may even be a specific artist behind the makeup effects. These individuals started with the most rudimentary skills and, through practice and repetition, have reached a professional level. Anyone can learn stage makeup skills and understand the building blocks of face and skin manipulation. The key is detailed instruction that is easy to visualize.

Foundations of Stage Makeup contains innovative teaching techniques designed to empower students with relevant makeup techniques meant to increase their skills and expand their knowledge. This book also presents material that supports instructors as they engage their class. The text can do this by utilizing three different areas of makeup education. The first few chapters discuss the basic building blocks of makeup education. The history of makeup shows how cosmetics have shaped cultures, and the chapter on sanitation and chemicals empowers students with tools to make wise product-purchasing decisions. Chapter 3 on facial anatomy showcases bone, muscle, and skin regions pertinent to makeup application. Two of the most important early chapters discuss color theory, light, and shadow, and their importance to makeup. Historical context is given to distinguish between light spectrums and pigment spectrums, and students will learn how to use the color wheel to choose appropriate colors for their projects.

The next several chapters build off this knowledge by describing actual terms and techniques about products and application processes. Modern cosmetics can be used as stage makeup, and these chapters showcase how these products work and how best to use them. Starting with preparing a performer's hair for a wig and moving through foundation, eyes, and lips, students will feel empowered with the information. They will be ready to start makeup applications in the following chapters now that they know the right tools to use and how to apply them.

Chapter 10 is the first makeup application chapter. Through Chapter 17, "Fantasy Makeup," students will learn specific applications for bone structure, masculine and feminine basic corrective makeup, and old age makeup. There are two emotion makeup chapters – angry and sad – along with instruction on numerous trauma and fantasy makeup techniques. The lessons learned in each section will build off the previous techniques and make learning them fun.

Students are not the only people to see fantastic makeups and want the knowledge to emulate them. Instructors can use *Foundations of Stage Makeup* as a definitive resource for their educational class. The beauty of this book comes with the online content and resources offered through the publisher. Video tutorials, available to instructors, demonstrate the following applications: wig prep, bone structure, basic corrective, old age, angry, sad, and trauma effects. I lead the multimedia discussion and demonstrate tricks and techniques on applying each makeup. Also online is the instructor resource manual. This document guides instructors through the rigorous process of setting up a makeup course and contains many example assignments for class use. The document also describes how to set up a challenging yet exciting final exam.

Stage makeup should not be a mystery. Performers, technicians, designers, and students should all have the basic tools to start developing skills for their profession. *Foundations of Stage Makeup* can do all this and more. I know it will be a welcome resource for any classroom.

CHAPTER I

A CONCISE HISTORY OF MAKEUP

ANCIENT EGYPT

The ancient Egyptians are the first people credited with the mass consumption of cosmetics. Men and women adorned their faces, bodies, and hair with makeup of various types and colors. Cosmetics were made from ground minerals and plants, and then combined with animal fats, oils, or water for application. Kohl is the most notable cosmetic of the ancient Egyptians. It was made from ground burnt almonds, manganese oxide, lead, or malachite. Green Malachite was the most popular shade for the eyes (Corson, "Fashions in Makeup"). Kohl was not only used as a heavy eyeliner, but a contrasting color was used as eye shadow. The Egyptians often painted their bodies with tinted ochre in yellow or orange hues and would use it as a rouge. Henna was also a popular cosmetic and would be painted on the palms of the feet and hands. It is interesting to note that cosmetics were made by the priests, and eye makeup was not just used for adornment but as protection from spirits and bad fortune.

ANCIENT CHINA

Emperors, empresses, and esteemed concubines set makeup trends in early Chinese periods. Rice, one of the most plentiful resources available, became the basis for many cosmetics of the time. Pale skin tones, especially on the face and neck, were the preferred foundation shades and could be achieved with rice powder or a mixture of toxic white lead (Chen, "How Cosmetics"). These pale tones were not mirrored by men, and men seldom wore cosmetics of any kind. Rouge colors were made from plant extracts and were often used on the cheeks as well as on the lips. In some instances, pig pancreas and cow pulp were used to thicken rouge mixtures as they were blended with powdered rouge products (Chen, "How Cosmetics"). Two types of products were frequently used to emphasize the eyebrows. Soot from chard willow branches would be used as well as a blue mineral called *dai* (Chen, "How Cosmetics"). In earlier periods the natural shape of the eyebrows would be emphasized, but in later periods the natural eyebrow was shaved and replaced with the desired shape.

ANCIENT GREECE

The modern term *cosmetic* derives from the Greek words for *cosmos* and *kosmetikos* meaning harmony, tranquility, and order. These ancient peoples sought to unify the body by creating their image of beauty through cosmetic products. Even though Mediterranean countries are sunny and warm, pale complexions were the desired shade for women. Women often employed white chalk or white lead mixed with water on face, shoulders, necks, and arms (Ancient Greece Facts, "Ancient Greece Makeup"). Pale skin was seen as distinguished and set society ladies apart from the working class. Rouge was used often and applied lightly to give a natural flushed appearance. The Greeks used many materials in their products like mulberry, seaweed, and various plant roots. Also vermilion, white lead, and red sulphide of mercury, called cinnabar, were used to color the cheeks and the lips (Corson, "Fashions in Makeup"). Eyebrows were colored black, and kohl or soot was often used to pigment them. It was desired to have the eyebrows meet in the middle, and if they were not drawn on then false eyebrows would be worn (Corson, "Fashions in Makeup"). Olive oil was a plentiful product and found its way into many of the cosmetics worn by women. It was used in massage and as a skin moisturizer helping to give the skin a youthful, healthy glow.

ITALIAN RENAISSANCE (1400–1600)

Cosmetics use in Medieval Europe was not widely practiced; however, with the emergence of the enlightened women of the Renaissance, cosmetics once again found their place in history. Given the extent of makeup use during this time, the lack of cosmetics variety is surprising. The most often used cosmetic product was foundation. Women desired to be as pale as possible, as a sign that they did not engage in manual labor. Ladies would use toxic substances, like white lead or mercury sulphide, to "white wash" their face, arms, neck, and chests (Corson, "Fashions in Makeup"). Often women did not remove the product from previous days but continually layered the foundation paste over the skin, filling any wrinkles. The pale, white color was bold and stark, yet it still appealed to society. Eyeshadow colors were frowned upon, while eyebrows were plucked to small thin lines. The only coloring to appear on the face was the occasional vermillion rouge on the cheeks and ears, with a slight coloration of the lips (Corson, "Fashions in Makeup").

ELIZABETHAN ENGLAND (1558–1603)

Queen Elizabeth I set the makeup fashions for this period of English history. Her makeup style was so iconic that most every woman of the era sought to emulate it. A pale complexion was already preferred by middle- and upper-class women, but the queen emphasized its need by continually lavishing it upon herself. The most popular foundation product for nobility was ceruse, a toxic combination of white lead and vinegar (Leed, "Elizabethan Make-up"). Other popular skin whitening methods included using a mixture of Borax and water, mixing talcum powder and egg whites, and using leeches to bleed the skin a pale complexion. Women would go to great lengths to make their faces appear even whiter by applying dark patches of cloth to their temples, dying their hair yellow, or using kohl or dark liner around their eyes (Corson, "Fashions in Makeup"). To make their skin appear translucent and naturally white, ladies drew small veins on the skin as well as used egg whites to give the skin a glazed sheen (Leed, "Elizabethan Make-up"). Vermillion was used to blush the cheeks and nose. This period is credited with the invention of the lipstick applicator. Small cylinders were packed with vermillion for lip application.

18TH CENTURY FRENCH STYLE

The French court saw several fashion trends come and go throughout the 18th century. Makeup, however, started bold and only grew bolder as the century progressed. Counter to the practices in England at the time, aristocratic makeup became heavier, while lower-class prostitutes sought a natural look. The foundation color, used by the aristocracy, was as pale as porcelain and applied so heavily that it often looked garish. Even though the toxicity level of white lead was well known and discussed, this did not discourage the aristocracy from using it. Upper-class men occasionally painted their faces as well, but the practice was frowned upon by middle- and lower-class society (Corson, "Fashions in Makeup"). A practice called patching was also common. The individual

would use small bits of fabric, cut in heart shapes, diamond shapes, and even the shapes of family and friends, to cover small sections of their face. Starting out as a way to cover pox marks caused by makeup poisoning, patching became so popular that often over half the face would be covered in patches (Corson, "Fashions in Makeup"). Veining, the process of tracing veins with color onto the skin, was popular as a way to make the skin appear translucent, and rouge was applied heavily later in the century. Vermillion and cinnabar were common products for cheeks and lips, while eyebrows were blackened or over-drawn. In some cases, eyebrows were shaved completely, and mouse fur would be applied for brows.

EARLY 19TH CENTURY EUROPE

The French Restoration and the advent of the Industrial Revolution saw the collapse of once held makeup standards. The pendulum swung the opposite direction and what had once been bold and shocking in intensity now became subdued and natural. Women tried to distance themselves from the 18th century era of opulence by gravitating toward light applications with familiar cosmetics. Complexions were pale, not because of heavy layers of foundation, but due to the use of rice powder and other lighter products (Corson, "Fashions in Makeup"). It was said that many husbands did not know that their wives wore makeup at all or at least pretended that they did not. Rouge fell completely out of fashion in the earlier part of the period. Older ladies still used it but drew criticism from publications and friends. This did not mean that rouge was never used; when used, cheek color had to look natural. The same standard was given to the lips as well. By the mid-19th century, women would be applying makeup in secret so as not to spoil the illusion of classic beauty.

LATE 19TH CENTURY

Opinions toward makeup changed in the latter half of the 19th century. Attitudes toward cosmetics use were divided into two camps of women: ones who painted their face and ones who did not paint (Corson, "Fashions in Makeup"). That is not to say that those who did not paint their faces did not wear cosmetics; it means that they did not want their makeup to be obvious. It was still the fashion to maintain a pale complexion, but with the creation of zinc oxide, foundation products were not always toxic. Women who could afford pearl powder used it to give their skin a light sheen. Often starch, lemon, and vinegar, or chalk were the recipes of choice for the complexion, but those were not as long-lasting as actual cosmetic products (Corson, "Fashions in Makeup"). Rouge had an interesting position in the late 19th century. Society ladies thought it was scandalous to wear because performers and prostitutes wore it heavily, yet many of those same ladies applied small amounts in secret. Rouge cosmetics came in three forms: cream, powder, and liquid. The liquid was the preferred method since it could give the most natural glow to the cheeks (Corson, "Fashions in Makeup"). Lip colors were made from natural products like rose water or wine as a stain rather than pigmented product. Eyebrows were blackened with kohl, India ink, or frankincense-

black, though the effect was frequently obvious (Corson, "Fashions in Makeup").

THE ROARING TWENTIES

Makeup became a household word once again. It was no longer applied in secret, but the use of cosmetics was expected of the modern woman. With the development of makeup counters in the previous decade, cosmetics were widely distributed and easy to obtain. The invention of the metal retractable lipstick tube and the hinged compact made cosmetic re-application easy, and the makeup was often applied in the open at restaurants and clubs (Spivack, "History of the Flapper"). Two things influenced American makeup trends in the 1920s. The first was the popularity of the silver screen. Film stars and celebrities became American royalty, and makeup styles used on screen made their way into the hands of eager women. The second thing to influence makeup trends was the 1922 discovery of the tomb of Egyptian boy-king Tutankhamen. The event was sensationalized and drove women to the makeup counters in hopes to mimic the Egyptian eye. Foundation color preference was pale. Toxic products were no longer popular. Rouge colors were red and orange and applied in circular motions on the cheeks (Spivack, "History of the Flapper"). Bold red was the most common lip color, and the desired shape was the *cupid's bow* made popular by actress Clara Bow. Kohl, in dark tones, was applied and smudged around the eyes, making the eyes appear bold and striking (Spivack, "History of the Flapper"). This decade saw the rise of the African-American, female cosmetics entrepreneur, such as Madame C.J. Walker, Annie Malone, and Sarah Spencer Washington. These women started tinkering with makeup in the decades before and mass-produced cosmetics intended for women with darker complexions (Summers, "Black Cosmetics"). The majority of products were intended to emulate the tone of paler women with skin-lightening creams being extremely popular. Another African-American entrepreneur, Madame M.A. Franklin, developed products that went beyond skin-lightening. Instead she offered women products to emphasize the natural skin tone.

1940S WARTIME IN THE UNITED STATES

World War II changed many aspects of American manufacturing and American demand for products. Nylon stockings, metal cosmetic cases, and various important chemicals were used in the war effort and unavailable to the throngs of women in the country. Despite these setbacks, the cosmetics industry saw higher sales than at any other time in history. On two occasions, the US government attempted to curb cosmetics consumption but realized it would have a significant financial impact on the economy (Corson, "Fashions in Makeup"). Pan-cake makeup, created by pioneer company Max Factor for the film industry in 1914, was available as a facial foundation and was even applied to the legs when stockings could not be worn (Corson, "Fashions in Makeup"). The company created several foundation tones not just for pale skin tones. In this decade it was acceptable for the face to be several shades darker than the natural tone, a contrast to the hundreds of years of makeup history previously.

There were more cosmetics colors than in years past, with the favorite lip tones being bright red, fuchsia, and orange to complement nail colors. Eyebrows were plucked and colored in high arches and were generally fuller than in the past decades. In the later part of the 1940s, women started using eyeliner, not only to emphasize the eye, but to create interesting shapes around their eyes like the *cat*-eye shape.

1960S IN THE UNITED STATES

There were three makeup movements of the 1960s – each distinct from the other. The first was a carryover from the 1950s, when housewives strove for a subtle elegance. Often referred to as the *classic* look, this movement was popular until around 1963. The colors and style were simple and relied on a sophisticated natural appearance. The matte powders of the 1950s were still used liberally to achieve classic beauty. Women used pan-cake makeup to conceal blemishes and achieve an overall less-is-more coverage. Classic looks were contrasted by the British movement in pop culture. Starting in the late 1950s and marching straight through to the 1970s, the most iconic makeup movement of the 1960s was the *mod* look. Influenced by fashion, people turned to bold expression to create their makeups. The eyes were the focal point, with emphasis on the eyeliner and shadows. Often false lashes were used on the lower lash line as well as the top. Black, white, and gray tones created a striking contrast with little color, while tones of blues and grays took the edge off harsh lines. Lip colors were pale, so as not to detract from the eye, and were often soft pinks or nude colored.

The last makeup movement of the 1960s started around 1967 and continued up through the 1970s. Labeled the *hippie* look, this movement saw a return to natural and earth tones. Gone were the bold patterns and flamboyant shapes of the years before. Natural lip tones with a hint of color on the eyes rounded out these makeups.

THE 1980S

With the mass production of magazines and the popular advertisers that came with them, makeup trends became global instead of regional. This decade saw fashions cross the Atlantic, from the United States to Western Europe. Pop singers and musicians were the biggest makeup influencers of the decade. With music videos and superstars on television and in movies, women and even men wanted to emulate the bold looks. The 1980s saw the cosmetics industry turning their marketing toward children and teens by creating colorful products that were fun to wear. Liquid foundation was the most popular type of foundation. It was applied heavily, not so much to create a certain color tone, but to create an even palate to showcase the bold eye colors, cheek colors, and lips. Foundation was set with heavy powder before other cosmetics were applied. *Rouge* was now referred to as *blush*. Blush was the most popular cosmetic used, bright pink being the color of choice. Women used blush to contour as well as color the cheeks, usually applying it in broad strokes from the ear down the cheekbone. The most popular eyeshadow colors were bright blue, pink, and purple. As with the lips, the bolder the better. Eyeliner was also heavy but usually concentrated around the outer corners of the eyes. Eyebrows were slightly bushier than in decades past and darkened. Lip colors were also bright and often glossy. Bold red, which was no longer the most popular shade, gave way to shimmering pinks and purples.

BIBLIOGRAPHY

Ancient Greece Facts, "Ancient Greece Makeup," Ancient Greece Facts.com, Accessed August 19, 2018, www.ancientgreecefacts.com/ancient-greek-makeup/

Chen, Cao, "How Cosmetics Were Created An ancient China," *China Daily*, April 21, 2018 www.chinadaily.com.cn/a/201804/21/WS5ada295aa3105cdcf6519a30.html

Corson, Richard. *Fashions in Makeup: From Ancient to Modern Times*. New York: Universe Books, 1972

Leed, Drea, "Elizabethan Make-Up 101," *Elizabethan Costume*, Accessed August 20, 2018, www.elizabethancostume.net/makeup.html

Spivack, Emily, "The History of the Flapper, Part 2: Make-Up Makes a Bold Entrance," Smithsonian.com, February 7, 2013, www.smithsonianmag.com/arts-culture/the-history-of-the-flapper-part-2-makeup-makes-a-bold-entrance-13098323/

Summers, Gerrie, "Black Cosmetics Pioneers," LiveAbout.com, February 16, 2018, www.liveabout.com/black-cosmetics-pioneers-2442513

CHAPTER 2

HYGIENE, SANITATION, AND CHEMICALS

HYGIENE

Stage makeup products are generally a heavier consistency than makeup used for everyday wear. The makeup has to emphasize a performer's features to thousands of people and last throughout a performance. The products come in thick, shear, and high definition varieties, but it is most often oil-based and called *cream makeup*. Another type of stage makeup is called *pan-cake makeup*, which is a dry, firmly pressed powder that needs to be mixed with water before application. Both varieties create a full coverage effect and can be highly pigmented.

For an individual who routinely applies makeup to his or her face, it is vital that steps be taken to ensure the face is kept clean and healthy. In later sections of this book, students will be instructed to conduct a daily skin care regimen to decrease breakouts. Many of the steps listed in the following sections are well known, but whether wearing daily makeup or stage makeup, they are good steps to keep in mind.

Morning Preparations Before Makeup Application

Step 1: Wash the face

It seems like an obvious first step, but the reality is that many people do not wash their face in the morning. If applying makeup on a regular basis, this is the first step to ensuring a healthy canvas. Keep the palette clean and free of natural oils and dirt that builds up at night. Makeup will look better if there are few blemishes to conceal.

Use warm or cool water to rinse the soap or facial wash off. Cool water works better because it makes the skin feel tight and fresh; however, warm water works together with cleaners to break up oils and dirt on the face. Whichever one is used, be sure to remove all cleansers from the face.

Step 2: Astringent or toner

There are three main categories of skin types; oily, dry, and combination. Before initiating a new skin-care regimen, one should determine which regimen would work best with his or her skin type. The next step of the pre-makeup routine is to identify if an astringent or toner should be used on the skin. Both products help to further cleanse the skin, but they have their differences.

Astringents are alcohol based. Different astringents include apple cider vinegar, witch hazel, or 70 percent isopropyl alcohol (see Figure 2.1). These products strip existing oils and grime from the face that washing does not clean. Usually applied with a cotton ball or cotton pad, these powerful liquids dig into the pores removing all oils from the skin. If the skin is naturally oily, astringents can be very effective. They are not recommended for individuals with dry skin as they can increase drying and cause cracking. Another perk of astringents is that they can tighten the areas around the pores. This helps to keep dirt and makeup from further entering the skin.

Toners are milder than astringents and not as harsh due to not having an alcohol base. One should use a toner to help rebalance the skin's

FIGURE 2.1 *Astringent products: apple cider vinegar, witch hazel, and isopropyl alcohol.*

Credit: Zeek Creative

natural ph level lost during washing (Villarreal, "Astringent"). Toner also works well for individuals with dry skin and tend to not create dry patches or flaking. Toners will not tighten the skin around the pores like astringents.

Step 3: Apply moisturizer

Once the skin is prepped, a layer of moisturizer should be applied. It is not recommended to do this while the face is dirty. Having a clean face, ready for makeup, ensures dirt does not get trapped under the layer of lotion. Daily moisturizing reduces the appearance of wrinkles while adding healthy vitamins into the skin. Skin is the largest organ of the human body and is very absorbent. Always select good quality, healthy products that enhance the skin.

When choosing the right moisturizer, find one strong in Vitamins A, B3, C, E, and K (see Figure 2.2). Vitamins A and E greatly reduce wrinkles and moisturize the skin while Vitamins B3, C, and K help even out the skin tone and remove color variants (Prevention, "5 Best"). Whichever one is chosen, stay away from lotions containing alcohol or acids. Many moisturizers contain these ingredients. Intended by manufacturers to kill bacteria, alcohol and acids will also dry out the skin faster, negating the overall purpose of the product and causing the consumer to use more.

The last benefit of moisturizer is its effectiveness with makeup application. Applying moisturizer at least an hour before makeup application allows it to soak into the skin, creating a barrier between the absorbent skin and the makeup. As skin absorbs whatever product is applied to it, moisturizer helps

FIGURE 2.2 *Moisturizer with Vitamins E, A, and D.*
Credit: Zeek Creative

reduce makeup absorption. Also applying lotion moments before the makeup application is not wise as the product will not have time to dry and will cause makeup application to be inconsistent and difficult.

Nighttime Preparations Before Bed

Step 1: Wash face

Often after stage makeup application, makeup is removed with makeup wipes, baby wipes, or cleanser. Even with these quick removal methods, remember that stage makeup is heavier than normal makeup. Significant effort may be necessary for removal, especially if using stage adhesives or eyebrow glue. Washing the face before bed cleans the skin before it touches the pillow, promoting a healthy face and eliminating the potential for additional dirt and grime buildup.

As previously mentioned, one of the most important actions a performer does is keep his or her face looking fresh. Face washing before bed removes all the leftover makeup particles from the day. For a production stage makeup could be applied on the face, neck, or ears. Many people forget about these little nooks and crannies only giving attention to the obvious facial areas. Be sure to remove all makeup so the leftover product does not sit overnight.

Step 2: Apply moisturizer

The same rules apply as in the morning application. Allow the moisturizer time to dry before heading to bed. There is no such thing as too much moisturizer especially when using a healthy product filled with nourishing vitamins.

Step 3: Pillow patrol

One of the most neglected parts of the regimen, but very important for any individual, is changing the pillow case often. Consider the following example:

An individual applied a makeup application in the morning and used a makeup wipe to clean

90 percent of the makeup from their face. After applying everyday makeup, they head out to complete the rest of the day. In the evening, the individual applies a little more makeup or some touch-ups to make the eyes smolder, then departs out for fun with friends. They get home late and, due to being tired, they collapse on the bed and sleep until morning.

In this scenario, all the makeup the individual wore was transferred onto the pillow. If they woke up the next morning, washed their face when they got up, and then washed before bed the individual would have followed a good facial cleaning regimen. What would happen when they laid a clean face on the pillow used the night before? The old makeup and grime from the day before would now be on the clean face digging into clean pores. This is called *contamination transference*, the transferring of bacteria from one object to another. Unless the face is cleaned each time it touches the pillow, the pillow will continue to transfer contaminants to the face. An unclean pillow causes many adults to break out with facial blemishes.

To cut down on this transference of oils and dirt, professionals recommend that pillowcases be changed once a week. This helps to cut down on the dust that naturally collects on objects and the oils and dirt that settle from unwashed faces. Keeping the pillow case clean keeps the face clean too.

SANITATION

Sanitation techniques are often overlooked by new makeup artists, students, and performers, yet sanitation may be the most important aspect of stage makeup. Keeping products clean and bacteria free not only maintains the integrity of the makeup but promotes healthy individuals. Contaminated makeup can lead to skin, mouth, and eye irritations while spreading contagious infections such as pink eye or cold sores. Makeup artists do not want to give clients infections or have a reputation for doing so. This makes sanitation techniques paramount in the professional industry.

The following list consists of basic techniques to keep makeup safe and hygienic. For professional or aspiring makeup artists, these techniques must always be considered. For the performer who only intends to use his or her own makeup supplies, some of the techniques may not be warranted. Utilize whatever steps are needed to keep the face, makeup, or industry reputation clean.

- **Wash hands before each makeup.** Clean hands are the first step in the fight against germs especially when working with multiple models. It not only eliminates contagions, but it sends a clear signal to the model that his or her health is a priority. Mental peace for models and performers is an essential part in the makeup artist's repertoire.

- **Keep hand sanitizer handy and visible.** If a sink is not readily available, then having a bottle of hand sanitizer handy is a must. For the mental peace of the model, consider applying it in front of them. This also tells him or her that cleanliness is important.

- **Use a spatula and palette.** There is one mantra that all professional makeup artists live by "Never double dip!" Double dipping occurs when placing a makeup sponge or brush in a makeup container then applying it to the model's face. If that same sponge, now contaminated with germs from the face, goes back into the makeup container the entire makeup container becomes contaminated. This example of contamination transference is especially easy with oil-based makeups and liquid makeups where bacteria can grow easily. To combat double dipping, use either a stainless steel or plastic makeup spatula to scoop out the product before placing it onto a palette. Popular palette types are stainless steel, plastic sheeting, or ceramic tile. Palettes are great for mixing colors and artists can work directly from the palette without compromising the makeup in the container. Both spatulas and palettes are a must when learning and working with makeup.

- **Keep materials clean.** This follows the same principle as the no double dipping rule. Whenever using a tool or instrument on the face, it must be cleaned. Disinfectant wipes, 70 percent isopropyl alcohol, or brush cleaner can all be used to clean tools such as eyelash curlers, eye and lip pencil sharpeners, tweezers, palettes, and spatulas. Wiping down spray bottles of alcohol and brush cleaner is also important. It is also necessary to keep the inside and outside of the makeup kit clean and orderly. Any way to achieve a professional atmosphere, one where cleanliness is a priority, will only help foster positive professional relationships (see Figure 2.3).

FIGURE 2.3 *Sanitize all makeup tools between clients.*

Credit: Zeek Creative

- **Use disposables whenever possible.** If working on multiple models, never use the same sponges, brushes, or tools for each one. Unless there is time to disinfect brushes and wipe down equipment, using disposables can help. Disposable mascara spoolies are one of the most important disposable products for makeup professionals. Often artists and performers do not think about mascara being infected, but bacteria grow easily in these small containers. Once the spoolie is used on one model, then it will infect the entire tube. Using a new disposable spoolie for each dip protects the integrity of the product and the model. The same principle can be applied to lipstick and eyeshadows.

- **Wash brushes often.** Clean brushes are the key to great makeups. After completing each makeup, brush care should always be performed. Multiple sets of brushes may be needed if the artists find themselves in situations where brushes cannot be cleaned after each model. When it comes to brush bristles, there are two types and each one can be cleaned differently. The first type contains synthetic bristles. These are plastic and effective with applying oil and liquid based makeup. Cleaning these can be as simple as using kitchen dish soap. The second type of brush bristles are ones made from natural hairs usually from various animals. Because of the cuticle, these are not good to use for oil-based makeups as they trap the product and make it difficult to remove. Natural hair bristles are best used with powder makeup. Cleaning these requires makeup cleaner or makeup wipes. Pour a little cleaner onto a paper towel or cloth then wipe the brush in the product. No matter how it is cleaned, always clean a brush before it touches another model's face.

- **Sanitize pressed powders.** It is difficult to scrape eyeshadows and power foundations onto palettes, so double dipping does occur. After using the product, one of two things can be done to sanitize. Use a facial tissue to lightly wipe off the top layer of the product. This removes the layer that the brush touched cleaning the makeup. Also spritz a light mist of 70 percent isopropyl alcohol over the product. Do not soak the makeup but allow a small mist to land on the surface. As long as the product is not soaked, the makeup will stay fresh and will not disintegrate. Allow the alcohol to evaporate before closing the container.

- **Sharpen makeup pencils.** Every time a pencil touches a face, it is contaminated. Between each model, spray off the tip with 70 percent isopropyl alcohol then give it a few turns with the pencil sharpener. This removes the top layer, sanitizing the pencil.

- **Keep colors clean.** Whether using lipstick from a tube or from a container, double dipping should never occur. Use a spatula to remove the product and place it on a makeup palette. From there it can be mixed and used directly. Scooping product also pertains to eyeliner products. On multiple models, try buying products which can be removed with a spatula such as gel liners. Stay away from felt tips and products that come with attached brushes.

CHEMICALS

Working with makeup means knowing what ingredients go into the products used. Professionals should be responsible in the purchasing of body products and makeup. Even though more companies are trying to "go green" many companies still operate from the 1950s mindset that chemicals in small doses are not harmful. It pays to be informed about chemicals and know how they can affect the body.

The first thing to understand, before purchasing products, is how cosmetics are labeled and who oversees the health requirements. According to the Food and Drug Administration's (FDA: United States (US) Regulatory Authority) official website, cosmetics and body products do not need government oversight. United States cosmetics companies are not required to provide lists of product formulas or register the ingredients they contain with the FDA (Food, "FDA"). Furthermore, the FDA does not require specific testing of body products and relies on the individual company for the information. What does this mean for US consumers?

The only entity testing and policing the labels of cosmetics and body products are the companies that produce them. Companies are not required to provide the name of every chemical on the label of a product, especially if those ingredients fall under the formula of *fragrance*. These are usually company secret recipes and do not need to be divulged. Terms like *all natural*, *organic*, and *herbal* also have no oversight in body products. In foods when a product says Certified FDA Organic you know that 98 percent of the product is organic. Such standards are not in the cosmetics industry. Anything can be labeled *natural*, but not be completely natural.

Cosmetic products often contain toxins, with harmful side effects, that may affect the body. The

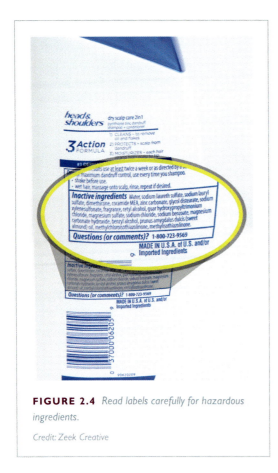

FIGURE 2.4 *Read labels carefully for hazardous ingredients.*

Credit: Zeek Creative

Cosmetic, Toiletry, and Perfumery Association in the United Kingdom, in conjunction with the European Union, identifies over 1300 chemicals and compounds as hazardous and bans them from being used by manufacturing companies that sell products in the UK (Official Journal of the European Union, "Regulation"). Many of these chemicals, used in large quantities, are proven neurotoxins, cause reproductive damage, or are known carcinogens. In the US, the total number of products and chemicals banned is around 14 with 11 of those being banned in the 1950s.

As professionals, it is important to stay informed on the products one is using. While it is true that extremely small doses of chemicals in beauty products can be safe, small doses are not what most consumers use. Daily use of multiple products creates chemical buildup and causes body toxicity levels to increase. Before buying cosmetics and body products based on brand name, investigate the ingredients.

BIBLIOGRAPHY

Food and Drug Administration, "FDA Authority of Cosmetics: How Cosmetics Are Not FDA-Approved but FDA-Regulated," Food and Drug Administration, Updated August 3, 2013, www.fda.gov/Cosmetics/GuidanceRegulation/LawsRegulations/ucm074162.htm

Official Journal of the European Union, "REGULATION (EC) No 1223/2009 OF THE EUROPEAN PARLIAMENT AND OF THE COUNCIL of 30 November 2009 on Cosmetic Products," Updated November 30, 2009, http://eur-lex.europa.eu/LexUriServ/LexUriServ.do?uri=OJ:L:2009:342:0059:0209:EN:PDF

Prevention, "5 Best Vitamins for Beautiful Skin," Prevention.com, December 11, 2013, www.prevention.com/beauty/5-best-vitamins-for-beautiful-skin

Villarreal, Raquel, "4 Things You Need to Know about Astringent," Livestrong, July 18, 2017, www.livestrong.com

CHAPTER 3

FACIAL ANATOMY

Stage and special effect makeup can be applied to any part of the body; however, for theatrical settings it is most often applied to the face. The face is the most visible part of the body. Most human sensory organs are on it, and it conveys human expression. Many individuals apply products to their face on a daily basis, yet they often do not know the anatomy of their canvas. The epidermal layer builds onto muscles, and muscles cover the bones. Learning the areas of the face is an important step in developing knowledge of stage makeup. This chapter presents three different diagrams along with labeled parts for each. These terms are important as they represent key areas where makeup is often applied, and they will be relevant later in this book. In the following sections are descriptions of these areas along with details on their significance.

SKELETAL

The skull is underneath each dermal layer of the skin and all muscle tissue (see Figure 3.1). The skull consists of 14 bones (Corsini, "Facial Bones"); most facial bones interconnect, but only one is mobile. For stage makeup purposes, eight are important to recognize.

The large, broad bone at the forehead is called the *Frontal bone*. This bone spans from the front of the crown of the head to the eye sockets. Usually smooth, it can contain brow ridges which help define masculine features from feminine ones and is often contoured with makeup. The *Lacrimal bone* is located between the bridge of the nose and the eye socket. This lacrimal region is above the lacrimal sac attached to the sinus cavities. Applying contour makeup here can increase expression intensity. Often referred to as the bridge of the nose, the *Nasal bone* is the ridge between the two Lacrimal bones. It extends down toward the nose hollow before ending. There is a sliver of bone that extends through the nose cavity called the *Vomer*. This bone travels through the nasal concha, the cavity below the Nasal bone, attaching the Nasal bone with the Maxilla. The last bone to remember in the eye region is the *Sphenoid bone*. This bone lies behind the eyeball and is hidden beneath the eye cavity. The Sphenoid bone will never have makeup applied on top of it; however, there are instances where the cavity can be represented on the epidermal layer.

There are two *Zygomatic bones* located under each of the eye sockets. The Zygomatic bones are also the cheekbones, and they can come in a variety of shapes. Sometimes rounded and sometimes angular, the cheekbones help define an individual's face shape. There is no end to the makeup effects that can be applied to them as they are easy to reshape with contour and highlight. Underneath the Zygomatic bones is the Maxilla. The *Maxilla* is the broad bone under the nose cavity containing the top row of teeth. Covered by the upper lip and mustache area, this bone is the immobile mouth bone. The

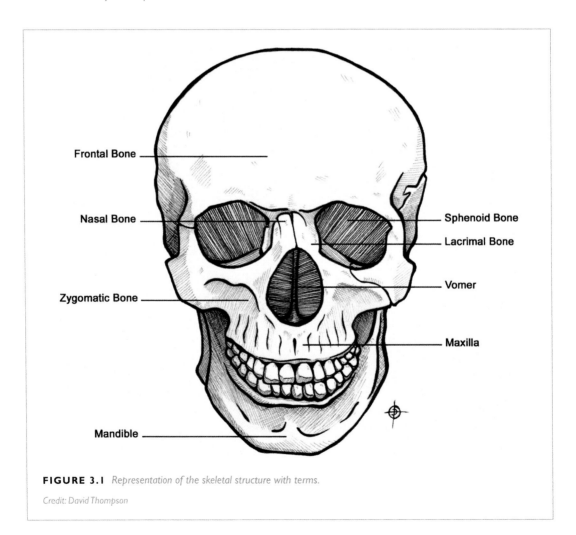

FIGURE 3.1 *Representation of the skeletal structure with terms.*

Credit: David Thompson

only mobile bone on the face is the *Mandible*. This large bone is also known as the *jawbone*. Essential in chewing and all mouth movement, the mandible can come in a variety of shapes. When shaped with sharp angles, mandibles can make a person's features appear more masculine; when shaped with soft curves, mandibles can make a person's features appear more feminine. Using makeup to reshape this bone allows for cross-gender applications.

MUSCULATURE

The entire muscle system is located between the skull and the dermal layer (see Figure 3.2). Without muscles, the human body could not move or function. Responsible for all facial expression and movement, the facial muscles can be manipulated with makeup to look like anything. There are 42 muscles in the human face (Eveleth, "Smartnew"). For stage makeup purposes, nine are important to recognize.

At the top of the face is the *Frontalis*. This large, yet thin, muscle travels down from the top of the head and overlaps the Frontal bone. It reaches down to the eyebrows before attaching to other muscles. The Frontalis allows the forehead to wrinkle when expressions are made. Below the Frontalis are two muscles attached under the eyebrows, the *Corrugators*. A single Corrugator is responsible for eyebrow movement and is key in expression creation. Angled diagonally under the eyebrows, these muscles are small in relation to the larger forehead muscle. The *Temporalis* is the thin muscle that overlays the temple area of the face. There is one muscle for each side of the head, and each one attaches

to the bone where the Frontalis lays across the skull. Contour makeup is often applied to this region to emphasize depth and create fantastical skeletal creatures. Moving down the nose, there is one muscle that spans the width of the nose. The *Nasalis* is the thin muscle overtop of the Nasal bone. It is thicker at the edges of the nose, and thinner over the actual bridge. This muscle aids in scrunching the nose and helps the nostrils to flare.

This next area of muscle covers a large circular area around the eyes. The *Orbicularis Oculi* is a layer of muscle that completely surrounds the eye. Various smaller muscles attach to the Orbicularis Oculi as they all help create expressions and help the eyes squint and close. There is another circuitous muscle on the face, but this one is located around the mouth. The *Orbicularis Oris* is an oval shaped muscle positioned around the lips. Like the Orbicularis Oculi, the Orbicularis Oris has many different muscles attached to it, aiding it in lip movement. This muscle also connects the Maxilla and the Mandible bones.

The *Masseter* is the powerful muscle connecting the Zygomatic bone with the Mandible. This muscle is instrumental in chewing and all jaw function. It can be felt most when the jaw is clenched tight, and the muscle is flexed. There is a small muscle directly on top of the ball of the chin called the *Mentalis*. This small muscle can be felt as the chin moves even though it is not the muscle that moves the chin. The Mentalis is a very thin muscle and attaches to the lower lip. The last muscle to discuss is actually a neck muscle. The *Platysma* is a large muscle connected to the Mandible which attaches to the collar bone. This strong muscle aids in neck and head movement. Stage makeup is often applied to

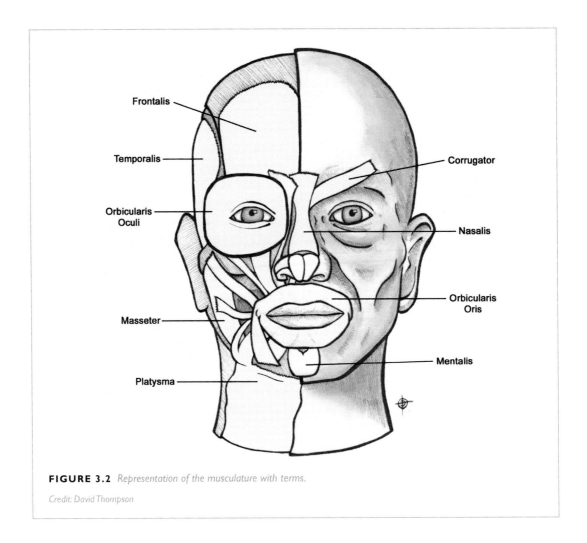

FIGURE 3.2 *Representation of the musculature with terms.*

Credit: David Thompson

this area as contour for the face and bones for skeletal makeups.

EPIDERMAL

The final layer of the skin is the most visual to the eyes. The Epidermal layer refers to the skin, the largest organ of the human body. Epidermis refers to the top dermal layer of the skin where dirt collects, and pores are located. The sun, wind, and environment can change the appearance of the Epidermal layer making it important to protect. There are a number of terms and regions to note on the skin layer. For stage makeup purposes, eight are important to recognize.

The small, slightly curved area of skin directly above the eyebrows is called the *Superciliary Arch*. This arch may bulge slightly from the skin around it adding to a masculine appearance. The eyebrow hair is at the bottom of the Superciliary Arch as this skin area does not drop into the eyelid area. Directly between the two Superciliary Arches is the *Glabella*. This area shows a human's concern when wrinkled. Contour and highlight can easily exaggerate the folds of the Glabella making it easy to use as an old age element. Below the Glabella on the bridge of the nose is the *Dorsum*. The

Dorsum directly overlays the Nasalis muscle and extends down toward the tip of the nose.

Under each eye is a pocket of fleshy skin called the *Palpebromalar Sulcus*. Usually in the shape of a half-moon, the Palpebromalar Sulcus is also called the under-eye bag. The term Sulcus refers to grooves, furrows, or trenches (Medicinenet, "Sulcus"). On the skin, it refers to the pockets of skin that may have grooves or

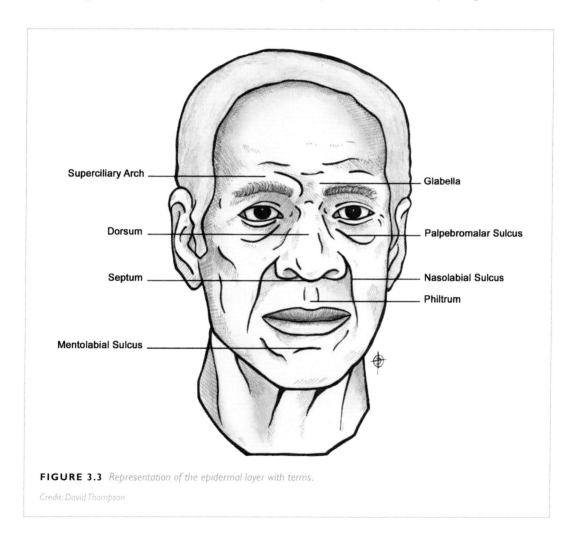

FIGURE 3.3 *Representation of the epidermal layer with terms.*

Credit: David Thompson

wrinkles around them. The Palpebromalar Sulcus is one such area as it is detailed by the wrinkle underneath the eye area. Another Epidermal feature also defined as a sulcus is the *Nasolabial Sulcus*. These two folds are located on either side of the Maxilla and extend from the nostrils down toward the corners of the month. The Nasolabial Sulcus gets deeper and more pronounced with age, so it is an easy region to emphasize with old age makeups.

Moving into the nose, the piece of skin that separates each nostril cavity is called the *Septum*. This area of heavy nose cartilage is slightly visible but instrumental as an anchor in holding down theatrical nose prosthetics. Underneath the Septum, directly on top of the Maxilla, is the *Philtrum*. The Philtrum is characterized by a small divot right below the Septum with two fleshy peaks on either side. It merges into the upper lip at the bottom and the Nasolabial Sulcus on either side. Finally, below the mouth, but above the chin, is a small fold called the *Mentolabial Sulcus*. Often contoured with makeup to change the appearance, this fold helps define the natural chin shape. It also lays overtop of the Mentalis muscle.

BIBLIOGRAPHY

Corsini, Dominic, "The 14 Facial Bones: Anatomy and Function," Accessed June 21, 2018, https://study.com/academy/lesson/the-14-facial-bones-anatomy-lesson.html

Eveleth, Rose, "Smartnew: Human Faces Might Only Express Four Basic Emotions," *Smithsonian*, February 4, 2014, www.smithsonianmag.com/smart-news/human-faces-might-only-express-four-basic-emotions-180949598/

Medicinenet, "Medical Definition of Sulcus," Medicinenet.com, March 19, 2012, www.medicinenet.com/script/main/art.asp?articlekey=5588

CHAPTER 4

THE COLOR THEORY OF MAKEUP

LIGHT AND COLOR

Makeup – whether for stage or everyday wear – is meant for two purposes: coverage and altering appearances. No matter the circumstance, using makeup will accomplish one, if not both of these purposes. Makeup cannot do that without pigmentation and color. Choosing the appropriate color palette for a particular project may seem simple on the surface but knowing how colors react and engage one another can make the task easier. Learning about colors – how to mix them, what to pair them with, and when to use a particular hue – is important and something of which every designer, artist, or performer should have a basic knowledge. Knowing these aspects of color is defined by the term color theory. *Color theory* relates to a set of color principles – how to make them and how they react with other colors. There is a wealth of information on this subject; however, this text will only focus on the rudimentary elements on the topic. Before learning about the use of color theory in makeup, it is important to learn how light, colors, and pigments are related and how they compare to other colors.

Before discussing pigments, understanding how light works is important. Physicist Sir Isaac Newton (1642–1727) conducted the first experiments into the complexities of light. Using a prism, he discovered that pure light is composed of seven colors: red, orange, yellow, green, cyan, indigo, and purple (Parramón, "Color Theory"). This means that all light from the sun, when passed through a glass prism, will break apart into these colors. Newton used a second prism to reassemble the colors back into white light, thus concluding that light was the source of all color.

From these early experiments with light and color, several primary color systems were developed. Physicist Thomas Young (1773–1829) made these first discoveries. Young took Newton's experiments with light and deduced that only three of the seven colors could produce white light: red, blue, and green. With just these three colors, white light can be achieved. This spectrum is called the *additive spectrum* (see Figure 4.1). When two of these colors combine, they add a new color to the system, a secondary color. The three secondary colors of the additive spectrum are cyan, magenta, and yellow. When green and red combine, they make yellow; when red and blue combine, they make magenta; and when blue and green combine, they make cyan (Parramón, "Color Theory"). The additive system is what most computer, LED, and televisions have in their screens. They are comprised of thousands of pixels and, when a combination of the three additive primary colors are mixed, form the multitude of colors conveyed to the viewer (Baird, "Why are").

The second set of primary colors makes more sense with pigments than light, yet it still ties into the additive spectrum. This system is called the *subtractive spectrum* (see Figure 4.2). The subtractive spectrum actually starts with the three secondary colors of the additive spectrum – cyan, magenta, and yellow. When dealing with pigments, it is apparent that artists cannot actually paint with light. When the three subtractive primaries are mixed together, they create black. Mixing two of each primary color together will also create the primary colors of the additive spectrum. When cyan and magenta combine, they make blue; when magenta and yellow combine, they make red; and when yellow and cyan are combined, they make green (Parramón, "Color Theory"). The subtractive spectrum also explains why the human eye sees

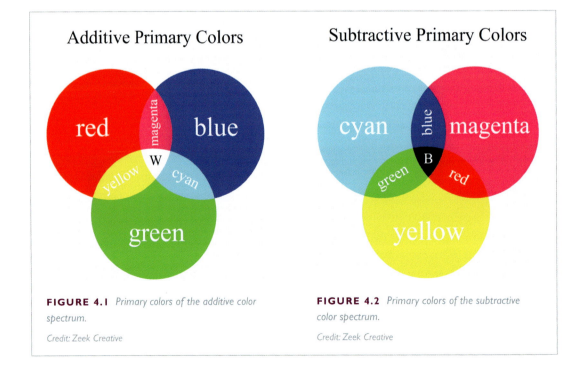

Additive Primary Colors

Subtractive Primary Colors

FIGURE 4.1 *Primary colors of the additive color spectrum.*

Credit: Zeek Creative

FIGURE 4.2 *Primary colors of the subtractive color spectrum.*

Credit: Zeek Creative

colors when viewing objects. As white light shines on an object, such as a lemon, all color is absorbed, or subtracted, except the color yellow. This color reflects from the object and is seen by the human eye. The same goes for every other color that is printed, created, or manufactured (Baird, "Why Are"). When black is the color being viewed, all colors of the light spectrum are absorbed into the object and none are reflected back at the viewer. The opposite is true for white objects; they absorb no colors and reflect them all.

Despite these two systems of color theory, there is one more that most people are familiar with and the one children are ingrained with since infancy. This system of color can be called the *artist color spectrum*. The artist color spectrum deals only with pigmented color and color products. The three primary colors consist of pure hues of red, blue, and yellow (see Figure 4.3). Little is known about why this became the universal color system, given the other two more scientific spectrums. Some suggest that the colors cyan and magenta are harder for children to recognize, and it is easier to identify them as blue and red. Whatever the case, for the purposes of stage makeup, this system of color is adequate in identifying the varieties of hues available to an artist or performer.

Now that the value of the artist color spectrum has been identified, several other aspects can be labeled. *Primary colors* are defined as any of a set of colors from which all other colors may be derived (Merriam-Webster, "Definition"). In the artist color spectrum, these colors are red, blue, and yellow. The additive and subtractive spectrums also have their primary colors, but — for the purposes of stage makeup — red, blue, and yellow

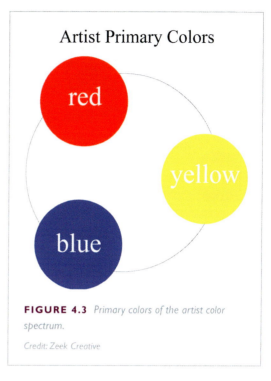

FIGURE 4.3 *Primary colors of the artist color spectrum.*

Credit: Zeek Creative

are the primary colors. No pigment can mix to create any of these three pure colors. When two of the primary colors mix, they create a *secondary color*. This is true for any of the three-color spectrums. The secondary colors of the artist color spectrum are green, orange, and purple where blue and yellow make green, yellow and red make orange, and red and blue make purple (see Figure 4.4). These three colors expand the color wheel giving an artist more options to use as pigments.

The artist color spectrum can be broadened again to include another group of colors. *Tertiary colors* are created by mixing a primary color with its related secondary color. The six tertiary colors of the artist color spectrum are yellow-orange, red-orange, red-purple, blue-purple, blue-green,

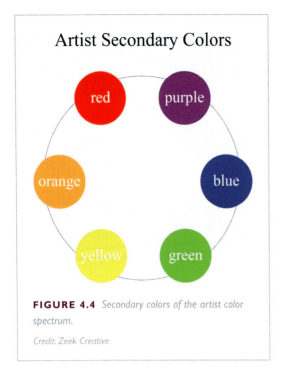

FIGURE 4.4 *Secondary colors of the artist color spectrum.*

Credit: Zeek Creative

and yellow-green. With the inclusion of these six colors, a completed color wheel can be created with twelve colors in all (see Figure 4.5). Of course, the color wheel could continue to be expanded with an infinite number of hues; however, for makeup purposes the 12-hue color wheel will suffice.

There are several more terms, concepts, and colors to discuss while examining the artist color wheel. *Complementary colors* are colors located directly opposite each other on the color wheel. The most obvious complementary color pairs are blue and orange, red and green, and purple and yellow. Paired together complementary colors contrast, yet complement, their partner. Design-wise they look good together, and many designers will pair them together in fashion and interior design. There is one requirement to have a complementary pair – they must be of

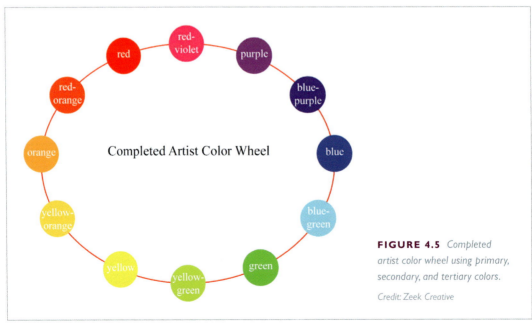

FIGURE 4.5 *Completed artist color wheel using primary, secondary, and tertiary colors.*

Credit: Zeek Creative

opposite color temperatures. Every color on the color wheel has a *color temperature*; that is to say they either feel warm or cool to the eye. Warm colors include red, orange, and yellow; cool colors include blue, purple, and green (see Figure 4.6). The color wheel can be split in half with cool hues on one side and warm hues on the other. When viewing the color wheel with two temperatures, it is easy to identify complementary color pairs.

There are two other important pigments that can be mixed using the color wheel. The first is the color black. Consider the subtractive spectrum. When the three primary colors of the subtractive spectrum – cyan, magenta, yellow –

are mixed together, black is achieved (see Figure 4.7). In essence, every color is mixed together to create black. It is the same with the artist color spectrum. Mixing blue, red, and yellow together will achieve a pure black. Altering the amount of any of the three colors will create a warmer black or a cooler black hue.

The second pigment which can be mixed is the color brown. To create brown tones, look to the complementary colors. A warm hue and its opposite cool hue must be present to mix an even shade of brown. Obvious color combinations are shown in Figure 4.8 and represent the most recognized complementary color combinations used to form brown – red

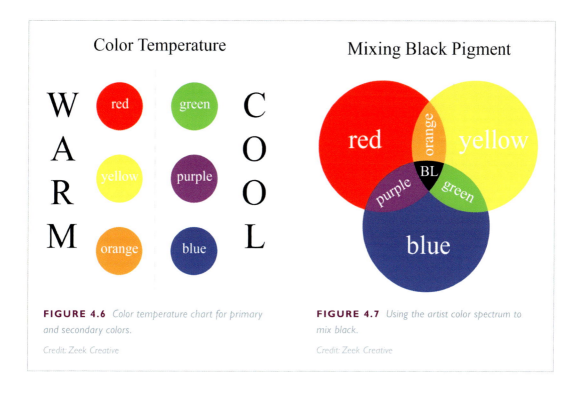

FIGURE 4.6 *Color temperature chart for primary and secondary colors.*

Credit: Zeek Creative

FIGURE 4.7 *Using the artist color spectrum to mix black.*

Credit: Zeek Creative

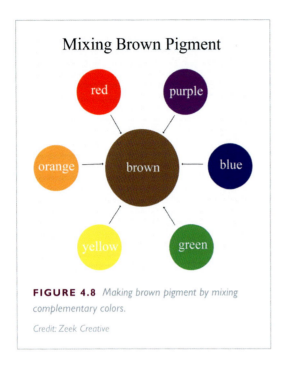

Mixing Brown Pigment

FIGURE 4.8 *Making brown pigment by mixing complementary colors.*

Credit: Zeek Creative

and green, blue and orange, yellow and purple. Increasing the amount of the warm color will result in a warmer brown while increasing the amount of the cool color will result in a cooler brown. Adding white pigment to each will create lighter brown hues such as sand or tan.

Now that the basics of color pigments are in place, several traits of colors should be discussed. The first is the concept of hue. The term hue has already been used several times in this text for its universality. *Hue* can be used as a synonym for color. Whenever the word *color* is used, it can be replaced with hue. Often colors that are mixed will have one primary color at 100 percent intensity. When that happens, the color is called a *pure hue* (Ames, "Color Theory Made Easy"). The primary and secondary colors

are the most obvious pure hues, but there are countless more. Hues can also be lighter or darker in color. This process is called value. *Value* is the lightness or darkness of an object. Say there is a red rubber ball sitting in the yard. The color of that red ball on a cloudless day with sunlight radiating onto it is the true color, called the *local color*, of the object. As the light fades and shadows deepen, so does the color value of the rubber ball. The value of the red ball's color will change depending on the amount of natural light.

Another aspect of color to note is intensity. When a color is at 100 percent saturation, it has *intensity*. Intensity can be low if the color is muted, or it can be high when a color is most brilliant or radiant. Bold colors have high intensity much like that red ball on a cloudless day. Intensity of a color can change when the value changes. *Tint* is when white pigment or lightness is added to a hue. The color gray is created when the tint of black changes and becomes lighter. *Shade* is the opposite of tint. When black or darkness is added to a hue, the shade of the color changes. The color gray can again be created changing the tint of white pigment and making it darker. Lastly the *tone* of a color changes when the pigment gray is added to the hue. Colors often look muted and dingy when the tone changes, but equal parts of tint and shade must be present for the tone of a hue to change

MAKEUP AND COLOR

A firm understanding of basic color theory is instrumental to excelling at makeup application. Every makeup product is pigmented with color whether it is a foundation product or eyeliner product. The key to finding the right color for the right person depends on knowing how colors react to skin and eye tones. The information that follows is useful for stage as well as in modern makeup application. For theatre, it could be that a historical period dictates the eyeshadow color rather than what is more complementary to the iris color.

Eyeshadows

Learning the color wheel can help designers, artists, and performers match and complement the natural eye color. Complement is the key word. If the eyes need to be expressive and wide, complementing the natural color will do wonders (see Figure 4.9). The good thing is that eyeshadow colors come in a multitude of hues and color temperatures. When choosing an eyeshadow to use, consider the iris color. The following list includes a few examples on how to match the most common eye colors.

- Blue is a very common eye color. If emphasizing the iris color is important, look to the opposite side of the artist color wheel. Blue's complementary color is orange. While applying an orange hue may not be favorable, copper and rust colors work to emphasize the blue tones.

- Green eyes can be darker or vibrant. Red is the opposite color on the artist color wheel. While using a bold red would certainly stand out, rust tones may more emphasize the green tones and be a more appealing design. Be certain that the color used has a reddish tone, such as maroon.

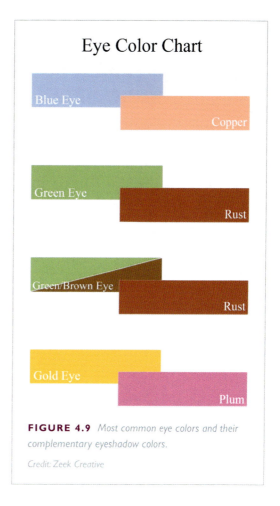

FIGURE 4.9 *Most common eye colors and their complementary eyeshadow colors.*

Credit: Zeek Creative

- Brown is the most common eye color, which works with most any eyeshadow color. Remember that a warm and a cool tone are used to create brown. If the iris is a warm brown, choose a cool eyeshadow tone; if the iris is a cool brown, try a warm eyeshadow color. The opposite temperature will make the iris color stand out more. If emphasis is not the intent, then any color should look good.

- Black or dark eyes have unique color. Due to the deep pigment, lighter colors will enhance the deep tone of the iris. Any color on the color wheel can be used, but if emphasis is the intent, lighter tones should be utilized.

- Hazel eyes can be multiple colors. Sometimes they are green and brown, or they can be brown and gold. Whatever their combination, eyeshadows for hazel eyes can be fun to design. Choose the color that will be emphasized, then look to the opposite of the color wheel.

- Gold or yellow flecks appear frequently in eye colors. They can appear in brown, green, and blue irises. To emphasize gold in the eyes, try using a purple, plum, or mulberry tone. Even a purplish burgundy will work, but ensure the hue has a cool temperature to best complement the gold or yellow.

Blush

Blush comes in beautiful colors, but there is more to choosing a blush tone than picking the prettiest one. To make an informed decision about color, the skin tone must be evaluated first. Most skin tones can be broken up into three categories; light, medium, and dark tones. They can further be broken down to makeup colors where pale tones are reflected in ivory to beige colors, medium tones are reflected in olive colors, and dark tones are reflected in bronze to ebony colors. Each skin tone range has a set of guidelines when it comes to wearable blush tones. The key to any blush tone is this simple rule: only choose a color that would be a natural flush tone of the individual. If

someone were going to run around the block and the face would flush, that is the color and intensity that looks most natural on the person.

- Ivory/beige tones: These colors represent pale complexions. Usually an individual whose skin tone falls in this range gets sunburned easily and may have freckles on the arms and face. Ivory/beige complexions look best with light pink blush colors – dusty rose, apricot, pale pink. Warm blush colors look best on ivory/beige complexions. These colors add warmth to pale skin tones; however, cool blush tones can work as well especially on very pale skin. Individuals within this skin tone range should stay away from dark blush colors like raisin or plum. These can give the appearance of bruising and will detract from the individual's appearance.

- Olive tones: These skin colors can be found in the Mediterranean region, Central and South America, as well as eastern Asian regions. Often persons with olive tones will become dark in the sunlight and do not burn easily. Individuals with olive complexions look best with mid-range reds. If a pink is going to be used, it should have a high color saturation level. Warm apricots to deeper reds are nice tones to use and recommended to complement the skin tone. Cooler tones do not accentuate the warmth of the natural complexion. Also, it is not advised to use dusty, pale pinks, deep raisin, or burgundy; these will also create a bruising effect.

- Bronze/ebony tones: These colors represent darker complexions. Individuals whose skin

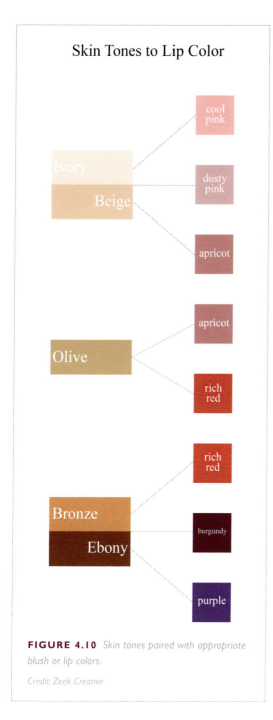

Skin Tones to Lip Color

(Ivory → cool pink, dusty pink; Beige → dusty pink, apricot; Olive → apricot, rich red; Bronze → rich red, burgundy; Ebony → burgundy, purple)

tones fall in this range take longer for a sunburn to become visible. Often the skin's natural color will deepen, and in some cases develop a warm glow. The skin's undertone temperature must be evaluated before choosing a complementing blush color. The skin can have a cool temperature or a warm color temperature. Try using a blush with the same color temperature to accentuate the features. Raisin, burgundy, or bold reds are nice complementing colors for bronze/ebony tones, while pale pinks and light reds can make the skin appear dry. Often a blush with shimmer in the product is best to use on dark complexions. Consider using gold shimmer instead of silver shimmer in blush products. Gold shimmer adds warmth and life to the skin, while silver shimmer can add to the dry appearance of the skin.

Lipstick

It is not necessary to reiterate the specifics of lip color on varied skin tones, as lip colors follow the same rules as blush. Lighter complexions should utilize pinks and mid-range reds but avoid dark colors. Olive complexions may use mid-range reds and some lighter red-purple combinations but avoid pale, cool pinks and purples. Darker complexions may use bold reds to dark burgundy but should refrain from pale, cool tones. Remember when evaluating what color to use, refer back to the artist color wheel. As noted at the beginning of this chapter, historical periods and show designs can also dictate lip colors that contradict these basic rules of color matching.

BIBLIOGRAPHY

Ames, Jim. *Color Theory Made Easy: A New Approach to Color Theory and How to Apply It to Mixing Paints.* New York: Watson-Guptill Publications, 1996

Baird, Christopher S., "Why Are Red, Yellow, and Blue the Primary Colors in Painting but Computer Screens Use Red, Green, and Blue?" Science Questions with Surprising Answers., January 22, 2015, http://wtamu.edu/~cbaird/sq/2015/01/22/why-are-red-yellow-and-blue-the-primary-colors-in-painting-but-computer-screens-use-red-green-and-blue/

Merriam-Webster, "Definition of Primary Color," *Merriam Webster Dictionary*, July 10, 2018, www.merriam-webster.com/dictionary/primary%20color

Parramón, José M. *Color Theory.* New York: Watson-Guptill Publications, 1988

CHAPTER 5

LIGHT, SHADOW, AND CONTOURING

Stage makeup fulfills many roles for the performer. It can change the color of the face, alter the features, and control expressions. The only way it can do this is through the use of contouring. Performers for stage should use facial contouring, just as models do for print, or actors do for film. Anytime professional lighting is used in theatre, film, or photography, makeup should be used. The amount of makeup can and should vary depending on the size of the performance space and the type of art medium. Knowing how light moves and how shadows fall over an object can help transform an otherwise flat canvas into a seemingly three-dimensional work of art.

A well-known principle of physics states that light does not curve. It can bend but usually needs an outside source to act upon it such as gravity (Cartwright, "Light bends"). This is a basic principle, but it has huge implications for stage design. Often lighting design and makeup design must work hand-in-hand. The lighting designer illuminates the performance space, influences scenic mood, and ensures the performers are visible. Stage makeup takes what lighting illuminates and makes it defined. Just as the scenery and costumes need to be visible by audience members siting in the balcony, so to do performer's features.

Consider the following scenario: a pale complexioned performer walks on stage in a dark costume. The stage is illuminated with lights shining from the sides, above the stage, and from the front of house. With his or her face lit from all angles, what happens to the face? Thinking about the direction of light and that it does not curve over surfaces, the performer's features would be completely washed out. The human face has natural curves and ridges. Dimensional lips, nose, eyes, and cheekbones all work together to tell a story. Multidirectional lighting can make the face appear featureless – a blank canvas. In the previous example, the pale complexion of the performer is another challenge. Once cool light tones wash over the performer, his or her face will shine in contrast to the dark clothing and can appear like a floating-head. These theatrical conditions should be evaluated before makeup begins. Makeup's role, in this example, is to put the contour and color back into the performer's facial features.

The process of using light and shadow to sculpt an object is called *chiaroscuro*. This is what lighting naturally does to objects, but makeup can achieve this as well. Using highlight and shadow colors, makeup can add depth to natural facial indentions or can accentuate the natural curvature of the features. Figure 5.1 demonstrates how lighting can affect two-dimensional objects. The first is a line drawing of a cylinder. Basic two-dimensional objects generally have little to no shadow or highlight. Shadows will only occur when an object is

illuminated by a distinct light source. The second cylinder in Figure 5.1 demonstrates how a flat object appears three-dimensional once light is shone onto an object. In this example, a light is shining directly in front of the cylinder. In the middle is the highlight where the object is the brightest. From there to the left and right sides, the shadows start light and then become deeper the further away from the brightest light point. Remember that light cannot curve around an object; light can only shine directly in front of the source of an object.

In Figure 5.1, the first cylinder has no light source illuminating it and thus no shadows; the second cylinder has one light source located directly in front. Taking this example a step further, what would happen if a cylinder has two light sources acting upon it? Figure 5.2

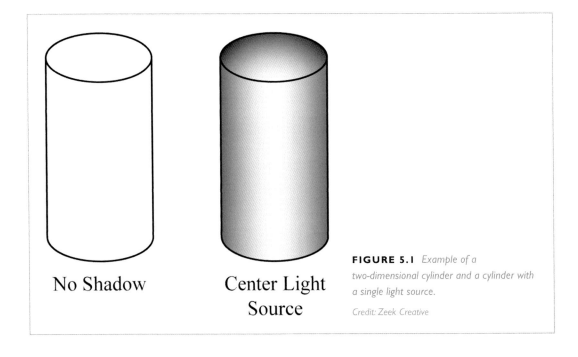

No Shadow   Center Light Source

FIGURE 5.1 *Example of a two-dimensional cylinder and a cylinder with a single light source.*

Credit: Zeek Creative

Center & Right Light Source

FIGURE 5.2 *Two light sources on one cylinder.*

Credit: Zeek Creative

of lighting. It is because of this that stage makeup plays an important part in design.

Stage makeup utilizes its own chiaroscuro effect, but instead of using light to shape an object, makeup uses color. Shadow colors – brown, dark brown, ebony – are used to add depth and dimension to the face. Highlight colors – beige, ultralight, golds – are used to attract light and illuminate high points on the face. Together shadows and highlights work to contour the face and to emphasis the natural three-dimensional features of the face. Without stage makeup, many performers' faces can appear flat and featureless. With stage makeup, expression can be achieved, and dimension attained.

Shadows are a natural part of any three-dimensional object, and the face is no different. Multi-directional lighting can eliminate many natural facial features. Adding shadow colors into the natural recesses of the face tricks the audience into thinking that lighting is doing all the work. Everywhere on the face shadow colors are applied, that area appears to recede or move back into space. Obvious places where shadow color can be applied for a basic stage makeup are in the cheekbones, at the temples, and around the eyes as eyeshadow. For good examples of these techniques, look no further than at the latest fashion magazine. Artists use makeup to give models angular cheeks and pointed jawlines. The same is true for stage.

illustrates the effect. By using the cylinder with one light source directly in front and adding a light source directly to the right, the shadows recede to the left of the cylinder. Now the complete right side and the middle are illuminated with highlight, and the left side is in shadow. Using this analogy, what would happen to a cylinder if three light sources of similar intensity were directed at it – one on the right, one on the left, and one in the middle? It would look very similar to the flat, two-dimensional cylinder in Figure 5.1. That is the power of lighting. Used effectively it can shape an object or rob it of its dimension. For the stage, this effect is often very real given the multidirectional use

Highlights are also a natural part of any three-dimensional object. Without points of intense light, everything would be hidden in shadow or in gray scale. Adding highlight tones onto facial ridges, near where the shadow is placed, tricks the eye into thinking the face has more dimension than it actually does. This is why old age stage makeup or special effect makeup is so effective. Wherever highlight is applied, those areas appear to project further out into space. Features like brow bones, Zygomatic bones, and chins all benefit from brighter makeup tones and aid in the illusion of a deeply contoured face.

To illustrate this point, refer to Figure 5.3. In this example there are two sets of three curved lines. These lines represent potential wrinkles on the face. The first set is three lines without any contouring. Perhaps these were naturally occurring on the face, but stage lighting has washed away all shadows and cast everything in highlight. Now consider the second set of three wavy lines. Notice that rudimentary shading has been added to the tops of the lines, while the highlight can be identified at the bottom of each line. In most every depression on the face, highlight is confined under the shadow. The light bathes the underside of these wrinkles before

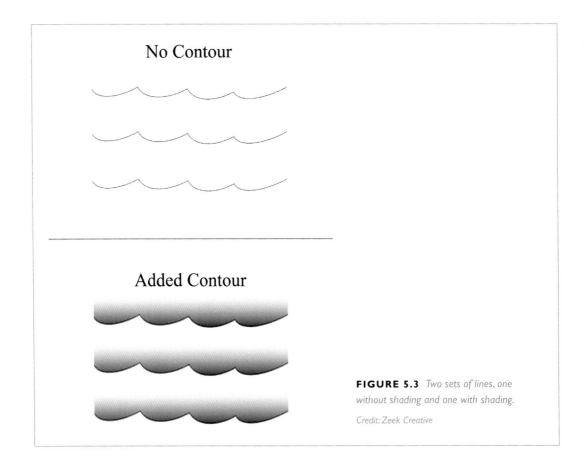

No Contour

Added Contour

FIGURE 5.3 *Two sets of lines, one without shading and one with shading.*

Credit: Zeek Creative

coming to an abrupt shadow. The shadow slowly migrates north before vanishing into light at the ridge. Just by adding this small amount of gradation to the illustration, the lines have become three-dimensional. To emphasize or create dimension, this is important to remember. Highlight color should be placed where light would naturally be found on the face; the same is true for shadow. Shadow exists in the absence of light. Dark contour colors may be applied wherever there should be lack of light. This example outlines an important principle in stage makeup. Whenever shadow color is applied, highlight color should be placed beside it. Shadow cannot exist without light otherwise everything is dark. When light is introduced, detailed shadows appear. If shadow is going to be applied as cheek contour under the Zygomatic bone, then highlight should be applied to the top of the bone. Adding the highlight will make the cheek appear more defined.

When contouring with makeup, think about it as painting on lighting effects. It is utilizing color to emphasize light that may occur naturally but is washed out by stage lights. Contouring is also about tricking the eye into thinking a feature exists that is not actually present. Creating contour with shadow and highlight colors takes practice and patience. It is not a skill that comes naturally to most people. Figure 5.4 exhibits

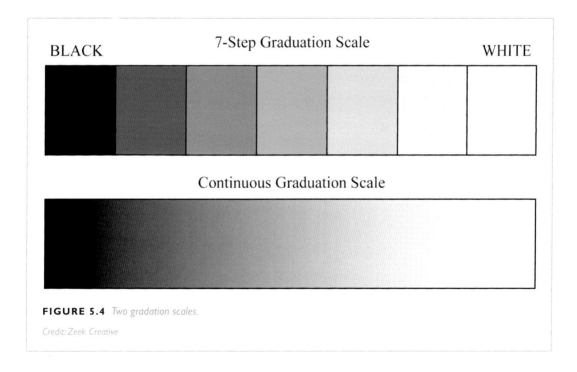

FIGURE 5.4 *Two gradation scales.*

Credit: Zeek Creative

two different shading scales. The first is a scale comprising seven rectangles where white is the lightest tone and absolute black is the darkest shade. The second is a gradation scale that moves from white to black through the layers of gray tones. To practice shading, consider taking some time to practice these two gray scales.

Learning how to shadow will make anyone more proficient at blending contour colors.

BIBLIOGRAPHY

Cartwright, Jon, "Light Bends by Itself," *Science Magazine*, April 19, 2012, www.sciencemag.org/news/2012/04/light-bends-itself

CHAPTER 6

WIGS AND WIG PREP

Anyone with aspirations for the stage or plans to work as a makeup or hair artist should have basic knowledge of wigs. At the very least, performers will, most often, be required to do his or her own wig prep before sitting down for a wig or their makeup. The term *wig prep* refers to creating a flat, firm surface underneath a wig by utilizing pin-curls, wrapping the hair, and applying a wig cap. Before discussing the techniques of pin curling and wrapping, several distinctions must be made when it comes to wigs and the tools used to work with them.

Wigs can be broken down into two fiber categories, synthetic hair and natural hair. Each fiber category has its pros and cons when it comes to use.

SYNTHETIC HAIR

Synthetic hair is essentially plastic. Each strand of synthetic hair is smooth without a follicle and without a root. It is manufactured to look and move like natural hair, and it is usually created to be flame resistant. Synthetic hair has different quality levels, however. The lower cost a synthetic wig is, the thicker and more brittle the fiber can be. Inexpensive synthetic hairpieces are often costume wigs sold around holidays and in children's costume packs. Such wigs should never be styled using hot styling tools such as flat irons and curling irons as the plastic will melt and burn. At higher costs, synthetic wigs are made with better quality plastic, as they are made to simulate natural hair. Hot styling tools may be used on better quality synthetics; however, they usually come with a warning to stay within a certain temperature before melting occurs.

Synthetic hair wigs hold their curl much better than their natural counterparts. Due to being plastic, steam is the best method to hold curl when adding rollers and setting the hair. Once styled, synthetic wigs will maintain the style even after they become frizzy on stage due to continual use. They are best used in musicals and long operas where performers either dance excessively or remain on stage under hot lighting and costumes. With frequent use the plastic fiber will break down and fray. When synthetic wigs are steamed and teased continually, they cease being useful and will have to be trimmed or retired.

NATURAL HAIR

Natural hair wigs are made from human hair or yak hair. Unlike synthetic fibers, they have both a follicle and a root. Human hair wigs are the most common type of natural-fiber wigs because the hair tends to be smoother and straighter than yak. Yak hair is thick, coarse, and must be heavily processed to become smooth like human hair. It reacts just like human hair, which makes it appealing for use in natural wigs.

Human hair wigs also come in different qualities. The less expensive wigs have hair that is more processed than expensive versions. Processing means the hair is chemically stripped of its original color and texture, then heavily recolored and permed to create a new product. These wigs generally come from South America and Asia where longer hair is more readily available. The hair color starts as dark brown and black, thus requiring more processing to achieve different colors. Better quality wigs are made from virgin hair, which is hair that has never been processed. Virgin hair wigs are the most expensive wigs available due to the materials being harder to obtain.

The good qualities of natural hair wigs are movement and reaction mimicking a natural head of hair. Unlike synthetic hair, hot styling tools can be used on natural hair wigs the same as a normal head of hair. Natural hair can be washed, brushed, curled, and straightened no different than an individual's own natural hair. Coloring processes can make natural hair any color, making them easy to match performers' own hair color. These two qualities make human hair wigs very appealing for film and straight plays.

WIG FRONTS

Synthetic and natural wigs can have one of two types of hairlines, a hard-front hairline or a lace-front hairline. The *front* is the area where the manufactured wig meets the skin of the forehead. The differences in the two can mean the difference between a realistic or stylized appearance for the character.

Hard-Front

Hard-front wigs are easy to recognize since the hairline is hard and straight across the forehead. They are typically manufactured in a factory by machine. As noted in Figure 6.1 the forehead line is sewn in a straight line with heavy fabric right up to the edge of the wig. These wigs are easy to identify especially if the hair is styled straight back off the forehead. In this example, the hard wig line is easy to see. Most often, when utilizing hard-front wigs, bangs are styled down on the forehead to conceal the edge making the wig appear more natural. Both synthetic and natural wigs can have hard fronts and most wigs are sold with a hard-front.

Lace-Front

Lace-front wigs have a piece of fine, mesh lace attached to the front of the wig. Hair strands

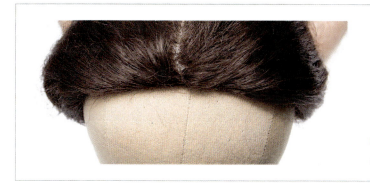

FIGURE 6.1 *Hard-front hairline.*

Credit: Zeek Creative

FIGURE 6.2 *Lace-front hairline.*

Credit: Zeek Creative

are tied into the mesh to simulate a natural hairline. The wig shown in Figure 6.2 shows the fine mesh and hair strands that are tied into it. Lace-front wigs are utilized in film, television, and in professional theatre venues around the world. Lace-fronts can be machine made, but the lace fabric tends to be thicker and visible when viewed up close. Lace-fronts can also be hand-made through ventilating. *Ventilating* is the process of hand-tying hair strand-by-strand into wig lace. Through the ventilating process, a wig maker can turn a hard-front wig into a lace-front wig. Lace-front wigs are more expensive than

hard front wigs due to the time spent adding lace and hair onto the wig.

WIG STYLING TOOLS

When applying wigs and creating a wig prep, certain tools are needed. Many of these tools are common, but all are important to remember. Following is a list detailing the tools used in creating wig preps as well as in styling wigs and hair.

- **2" hair pin**: small pin used to secure a wig cap to pin-curls (used in wig styling)

- **3" hair pin (wig pin)**: large hair pin used to secure light and medium weighted wigs to wig prep (used in wig styling)

- **Geisha/Amazon pin**: the largest sized hair pin, often 4'' long (used to secure heavy wigs to wig prep)

- **bobby pin**: small pin with two synching sides; one side is flat and the other is usually ridged (used to secure two hair sections together)

- **"T" pin**: a thin pin shaped like the letter "T" with a sharp pointed end; not for use on human heads (used to secure wigs onto a canvas or Styrofoam wig block)

- **rattail comb**: a styling utensil with a comb on one end and a long thin point at the other end (used in styling wigs and hair)

- **5-prong comb**: a styling utensil with a comb on one end and a small 5-prong pick at the other; the comb end has little ridges inside the tines which aid in back-combing (used for wig and hair styling)

- **wig cap**: a nylon cap that covers pin-curls before a wig is applied

- **medical bandage**: a length of ace bandage used to wrap injuries (used as a head wrap for short hair wig prep)

- **wig block**: a canvas stand to hold wigs when styling; usually made of canvas and filled with sawdust or cork (the best place to keep a styled wig during a production)

- **pop clips**: small clips generally used in styling; clips snap together and are useful to secure the bandage to itself for a short hair wig prep

- **duckbills**: thin clamps that secure hair temporarily while styling

WIG PREP VARIATIONS

A performer must secure their hair before wearing a wig for a show. By preparing the performer's hair, a wig prep ensures a solid base on which to hold the wig. When starting the pin-curl process, remember to keep the hair as flat to the scalp as possible. A flat wig prep ensures lumps of the performer's hair are not visible under the wig, thus altering the shape of the head. In the following sections are four methods for preparing an individual's hair for a wig, depending on the length and texture of the hair.

Method 1: Short Length

Short length hair may be like men's styled hair, short on the sides and long on the top. It may also be short textured women's styles – pixie cuts and tight backs with long sides and front. Any hair style five inches or shorter can be considered short length. A special way of securing a wig prep is detailed as follows.

Take a small section of hair at the front of the hair line and twist it into a nub. Using bobby pins, secure the nub in place. If the hair is long enough, try to do the same thing to the sides above the ears. If this cannot be done, then move onto the next step.

Measure out a length of medical bandage that can wrap around the head. Wrap it around the perimeter of the hairline and secure the ends with crisscrossed bobby pins or pop clips. Now use pop-clips to secure the bandage to the hair if possible. The preferred places to put the clips are over the sideburn areas and at the two points at the nape (see Figure 6.3). This will be difficult given the length of the hair but use the clips to

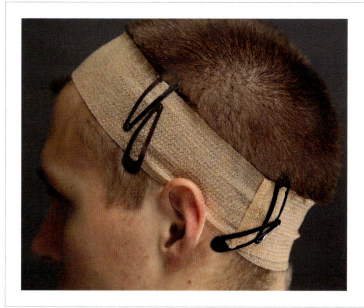

FIGURE 6.3 *Short-hair head wrap using bandage and clips.*

Credit: Zeek Creative

grab as much hair as possible. Use a rattail comb to push stray hairs under the bandage. Next, apply a wig cap over the head so that the edges cover the perimeter of the bandage. Using five hairpins, push them through the wig cap and under each of the pop clips. This will keep the wig cap and the bandage from sliding, creating a solid wig base.

Method 2: Medium Length

Knowing how to make pin-curls is essential when doing a solid wig prep. They can be difficult on first attempt, but with practice pin-curls become easier (see Figure 6.4). Medium length hair is longer than five inches and stops below the shoulders. The following steps describe how to achieve a solid wig prep for medium length hair.

Start by selecting a 2" × 2" section of hair at the center front of the head. With two fingers positioned at the base of the hair, gently wrap the hair around the two fingers. When the hair is wrapped completely, place the tips of the fingers onto the scalp and slide the hair off and into a circular curl. Lastly take two bobby pins and crisscross them holding the pin-curl in place. This is the first pin-curl (see Figure 6.4).

There are three important locations to place pin-curls – one pin-curl above each sideburn, the central one at the forehead, and two over each point of the nape. Once you have these five positioned, the rest of the head can be pin-curled into any pattern. These five pin-curls are essential in keeping the wig secured to the head, so they are the most important. The other pin-curls are only meant to contain the hair. They should be solid, but the positioning is not important (see Figure 6.5).

After the pin-curls are finished, take a wig cap and place it over the hair. The front of the hairline should show about half an inch at the forehead but make sure the wig cap is not pushed too far back. Use a rattail comb and wig cap as described in the Short Hair section to finish off the wig prep (see Figure 6.6).

FIGURE 6.4 *Two-finger method for creating pin-curls.*

Credit: Zeek Creative

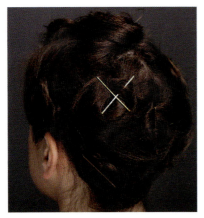

FIGURE 6.5 *Completed pin-curls.*

Credit: Zeek Creative

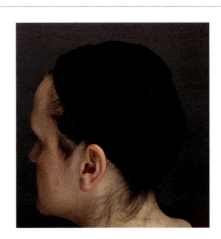

FIGURE 6.6 *Completed wig prep.*

Credit: Zeek Creative

Method 3: Long Length

If the hair is longer than shoulder length, it is considered long. For long styles, the wig prep should consist of pin-curls and a technique called wrapping described as follows.

To start, select a 2" × 2" section of hair at the front of the head (see Figure 6.7). With two fingers positioned at the base of the hair, gently wrap the hair around the two fingers. When the hair is wrapped completely, place the tips of the fingers onto the scalp and slide the hair off and into a circular curl. Lastly, take two bobby pins and crisscross them holding the pin-curl in place. This is the first pin-curl.

With long hair, only three pin-curls are needed around the hairline. One in the middle of the forehead and one over each sideburn. Now move to the crown of the head and create one large pin-curl 3" × 3" with a section of hair.

FIGURE 6.7 *Front pin-curls for long hair.*

Credit: Zeek Creative

FIGURE 6.8 *Sections for hair wrap.*

Credit: Zeek Creative

FIGURE 6.9 *Completed prep for long hair.*

Credit: Zeek Creative

section and wrap it around the head counter-clockwise placing the large pin-curl, at the crown of the head, at the center of the wrap. Secure this hair down with as many bobby pins as needed. Next, take the large right section and wrap it clockwise around the large pin-curl at the crown of the head. Then secure it with bobby pins. This is the head wrap. Lastly, create the two, small pin-curls at the nape.

After the pin-curls are finished, take a wig cap and place it over the hair. The front of the hairline should show about half an inch at the forehead, but make sure the wig cap is not pushed too far back. Use a rattail comb and wig cap as described in the Short Hair section to finish off the wig prep (see Figure 6.9).

Method 4: Textured Hair

Sometimes performers in need of a wig have naturally textured hair. Textured hair can be

The remaining hair can now be split into three sections (see Figure 6.8). Using one finger, slide it horizontally two inches above the nape. This section of hair will be used to make two pin-curls at the nape. There is now a large section of hair in the middle of the head. Divide this section vertically down the middle making two equal sized sections. First take the left

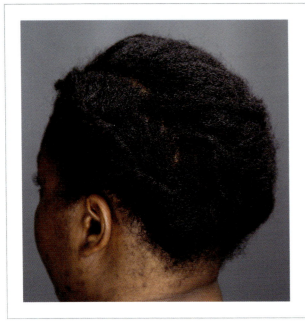

FIGURE 6.10 *Example of twisting method for textured hair.*

Credit: Zeek Creative

described as curly, kinky, coarse, or wavy. Trying to get textured hair as flat as possible can be achieved using a variety of the methods mentioned previously; however, when the hair is thick, pin-curls may not be necessary as the texture acts as its own locking mechanism. In this case, rolling the hair around the perimeter of the head and securing the ends at the back or at the crown of the head are both acceptable methods. Braiding can also be used to contain the hair and cinch it closer to the scalp. Two to three French braids woven around the head will ensure that the textured hair stays tight (see Figure 6.10).

Whichever method you use to prepare textured hair, be sure to keep the natural shape of the head in mind. The human head is generally thinner on the sides with the occipital lobe at the back. When doing a wig prep, try to maintain the general shape of the human head by concentrating the bulk of hair at the natural curves of the skull. This will enhance the illusion that the wig is actually real hair.

After the pin-curls are finished, take a wig cap and place it over the hair. The front of the hairline should show about half an inch at the forehead, but make sure the wig cap is not pushed too far back. Use a rattail comb and wig cap as described in the Short Hair section to finish off the wig prep.

WIG APPLICATION

Once the wig prep is complete, it is time to secure the wig. After the wig has been placed into position four wig pins will be needed. Pretend that at the crown of the head there is a spot. All the wig pins should point to that spot. Remembering

FIGURE 6.11 *Inserting front wig pin about sideburn.*

Credit: Zeek Creative

FIGURE 6.12 *Inserting back wig pin in nape pin-curls.*

Credit: Zeek Creative

where the two sideburn pin-curls and the two nape pin-curls are placed, carefully slide a wig pin through the base of the wig and into each of the pin-curls. Make sure the end is still pointing toward the "spot." The performer should be able to feel the wig pin pass through the pin-curl or underneath it (see Figures 6.11 and 6.12).

Be sure to not force the pins through the wig into the wig prep. Pins are sharp and can scrape the head causing bleeding. To minimize scrapes, put fingers under the wig and poke the wig pin into the fingers, not directly into the pin-curl. Once the pin has punctured the wig, slide the pin along the fingers and into the pin-curl. Once all four wig pins have been applied and are pointing to the center "spot" then the wig is secured. If it appears that more pins are needed, discreetly slide them through the wig around the

FIGURE 6.13 *Using a brush to apply adhesive under lace.*

Credit: Zeek Creative

perimeter and into the top of the wig. Be sure to catch pin-curls in the wig prep or the pins will be ineffective.

If a lace-front wig is being used, a theatrical adhesive may be necessary to keep the front lace flat to the skin. When applying theatrical adhesive, brush the product onto the skin under the lace then gently pat the lace down onto the skin. Once dry, the adhesive should create a firm hold that will last through most performances.

CHAPTER 7

FOUNDATION AND CONCEALER

Facial evaluation is key to any application, and due to its importance, it will be discussed several times throughout this book. Before makeup can be applied to the face, evaluation of the surface must first be performed, and several questions should be asked. *What is the intrinsic color of the skin? What is the color temperature? Are there uneven tones which need to be corrected? Are there irregularities on the skin which will detract from the desired makeup application?* Concealer and foundation work to create a strong base before the first application of makeup.

CONCEALER

The first step of any makeup application is to decide if concealer is needed. If the makeup application is supposed to be rugged or if the character is aged, concealing techniques may not be necessary. In many cases, however, concealing is the initial building block to great makeup projects. Being knowledgeable of color theory

will help determine what colors lie within the skin and, more importantly, how to correct the irregularities.

Along with determining what needs to be corrected, determine what product will be used to conceal the element. Cream makeup concealers are usually best for covering intense spots on the face. With the higher pigment and thicker consistency, cream makeup is easy to apply and quick to cover the surface. If multiple applications are needed, a little setting powder between applications will increase the concealing effectiveness. Powder concealers tend to be sheer in application. They can often cover light areas of color on the face but are not effective at achieving maximum concealing coverage.

Irregularities on the face can manifest themselves in many ways. They could be brightly colored in small intense areas or they could be larger areas of the face in light washes of color. Determine what needs to be corrected, then work to correct the colors. The most common elements needing concealing are blemishes, dark circles, moles, and birth marks.

A. **Blemish**: A blemish is any spot on the face that is red or pink in color (see Figure 7.1). Reds are generally warm tones; however a blemish which is pink can have a cool undertone. Determine which color temperature needs to be concealed, then choose a makeup product to use.

- In reference to the color wheel, to neutralize a color temperature, the opposite temperature should be used. Red is generally a warm tone, so a cool tone can be applied to neutralize the warmth. Green is the opposite color on the color wheel, so using it to cover a warm blemish is preferred. This does not mean that a bright or bold green should always be used. If the blemish tone is intense then the concealing tone should be intense; if the blemish tone is muted, then so can be the concealing tone.

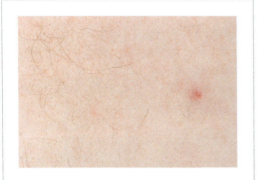

FIGURE 7.1 *Blemish with pink undertone.*
Credit: Zeek Creative

- If a green tone is not available, using a concealer color with a cool temperature can also be effective. Flesh-tone concealers have their own color temperatures. Choosing a flesh-tone with a very cool tone, but still one that matches close to the skin foundation color, will also work to neutralize a blemish.

B. **Dark circles**: Depending on the skin tone, dark circles can be a combination of cool colors. Often blue, navy, and violet on fair skin or violet and browns on darker complexions, the under-eye areas are some of the most obvious places to conceal. These dark colorations can be due to lack of sleep, stress, or even heredity. Before diving into concealment, first evaluate the colors needing to be covered and the color temperature required to neutralize the tones.

- If the majority of the dark circle is blue or violet (see Figure 7.2), look to the opposite side of the color wheel for the tone to conceal them. Orange or warm foundation colors will neutralize the cool blue and purple tones. Remember the concealing tone can be strong if the discoloration on the face is strong. Using a warm or orange-tinted foundation will also work before applying powder to set the concealer.

- If the dark circle has more brown or dark tones (see Figure 7.3), then evaluate the color temperature. Are the brown tones warm or cool? Whichever one is present, use the opposite temperature to conceal it. It may be that using the tinted foundation color works best to conceal these dark circles.

FIGURE 7.2 *Example of blue/violet under-eye coloration.*

Credit: Zeek Creative

FIGURE 7.3 *Example of brown tones under the eye.*

Credit: Zeek Creative

C. **Moles and birth marks**: Moles and birth marks can be tricky to conceal. They are often brown (see Figure 7.4), and brown is not found on the typical color wheel. In fact, to create a brown tone two complementary colors with opposite color temperatures must be mixed together. The good thing is that most browns have an intrinsic color. First, figure out

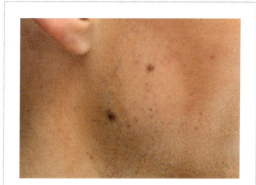

FIGURE 7.4 *Example of brown coloration in moles.*

Credit: Zeek Creative

what the undertone of the mole or birth mark is before choosing a color to correct it.

- If the mark has a cool bluish undertone, then applying a heavy orange concealer cream will work to neutralize the tone.

- If the mark has a warm reddish or pink undertone, applying a heavy green concealer cream will neutralize the tone.

In both instances, heavy powder followed by the foundation product should take the mole or birth mark away. Be sure to blot the foundation color so as to not disturb the concealer tone underneath.

FOUNDATION

Evaluating Skin and Products

Once all the skin irregularities have been corrected, apply the foundation. Before the first application, there are several things to evaluate. First, figure out the skin's undertone. The *undertone* is the intrinsic, or underlying, color of an object; in this case, the skin. Every face has an intrinsic color; for some it can be pink or red; it can also be yellow or golden, and blue in darker complexions.

Next, choose a foundation color that coincides with the undertone of the skin. In most cases, matching the undertone looks the best; however, in many performance instances lighting will have an effect on the makeup. Choosing a foundation tone that supports the lighting may also need to be calculated. Along with this, determine if the performer should have a foundation matching his or her skin tone, a shade or two darker, or a shade or two lighter. There are instances, laid out in later chapters, where changing the skin tone could be preferable. Be thinking about this while determining foundation color. Also, remember that for lighting designs, many follow-spots use cool tones. Going too pale with a foundation will make a performer appear deathly ill or appear grayish in tone.

Lastly, consider which foundation medium will be used. There are three types of foundation mediums, each has its positive and negative attributes. Knowing which one to use in the appropriate situation is key to a complete makeup application.

A. **Powder**: Powder foundations are nice for several reasons. Many powder foundations are hypo-allergenic and can be easier on sensitive skin. This makes them a good choice for many individuals. Powders offer a light application over the skin and give a sheer coverage, which is great if the individual already has unblemished skin. They can also come in several finishes. A *finish* is how the skin looks after the makeup is applied – dry, natural, or shimmery. The available finishes for powder foundations are matte and shimmery. The downside of using powder foundations is they do not offer full coverage and do not work well on skin needing irregularity correction. Given its sheer coverage, powders do not work as well as concealer products, and they do not work well as a stage foundation product.

B. **Cream**: Cream foundations are the opposite end of the makeup spectrum from powder foundations. Creams offer the most coverage of any foundation product due to their thick consistency and heavy pigmentation. That is why they make the best concealer products. Creams can be blended easily together to create a desired skin tone and have the durability to last for hours on end. Higher end cream foundations can offer a sheer coverage; however, creams are more likely to disrupt the natural pH in the skin. Due to the heavy consistency, individuals are more prone to temporary breakouts unless regular skin care is observed. The finishes available to cream foundations are matte and natural. If cream foundations are not set with loose powder and fixer spray, they will smear. The loose powder gives cream makeup a matte finish, but creams with added shimmer can be used to counter this effect. For the stage, cream foundations are a good choice because they allow for optimal blending of colors.

C. **Liquid**: There are a couple different types of foundations categorized as liquid. The first is a product purchased in a tube or bottle in liquid form. The second is a dry product, called pan-cake foundation, which requires adding water before skin application. When describing liquid foundations, both products fall under this category. Liquid foundations are the medium product between powder and cream. They can be used as a sheer application or can be applied heavier like a cream. Many brands offer a full-coverage product, though they are not as heavy a coverage as cream makeup. For achieving dewy, natural, or shimmery finishes, liquids offer a wide selection of products. Liquid foundations can also disrupt the natural pH in the skin, so regular skin care should be observed while using them. It is difficult to blend foundation colors. Once they are applied to the skin, it can be difficult to manipulate makeup colors on top of them. They can be a nice choice for theatrical performers if used as a basic makeup application.

Foundation Color Matching for Dark Complexions

Performers with skin tones ranging in the bronze, ebony, and chestnut families must have the skin evaluated in different ways (see Figure 7.5). Unlike in fair complexions, darker tones often have rich, golden hues as natural highlights and darker hues as natural shadows. Choosing just one foundation color to cover the entire face can

FIGURE 7.5 *Dark skin tone before foundation application.*

Credit: Zeek Creative

leave the features lifeless and dull. Often single-toned foundations will look unnatural on darker complexions.

When evaluating skin tones, choose different colors for the appropriate areas of the face. If there are golds on the cheeks, do not cover them with dark browns. Play into the natural coloring of the areas by using tones that reflect the natural color (see Figure 7.6), not a general color for the whole face. This will create naturalism in the makeup and cause the makeup to look fresh and vibrant. Once an appropriate color combination is determined, consider writing it down for reference in future makeup applications.

FIGURE 7.6 *Golden tones used in foundation application.*

Credit: Zeek Creative

General Application

Using a latex-free makeup sponge, apply foundation color over the face starting at the forehead and working down toward the neck. If concealer was used, dab foundation over these areas as not to disrupt the concealing product underneath. Foundation color should be applied to the jawline and blended down onto the neck. If the natural foundation color was chosen, there should be very little difference between the color of the neck and the color of the face. In some cases, the ears will be redder or seem discolored from the face. Apply a light coat of foundation to the ears if necessary.

When using liquid or cream makeup products, it is essential to set the makeup with loose or pressed translucent powder. Without powder, cream makeup will run and get on costumes and other performers. For stage makeup, cloth powder puffs are the best choice over large powder brushes. Cloth puffs allow the powder to get firmly pressed into the face and makeup whereas powder brushes deliver only a light application of product and do not firmly apply the powder.

To apply powder, deposit a generous amount onto a napkin or palette. If using a pressed powder, the product can be used directly from the container. Take the cloth powder puff and press it firmly into the product. Knock the excess powder off the puff so as not to deposit a large amount at once. With the cloth puff loaded with product, firmly dab the powder everywhere foundation was applied. These are quick blots made all around the face. Once completed, the makeup should be set and ready for shadowing and highlighting. If there is excess powder on the face, a large powder brush may be used to brush away the excess. Also, if the performer is already wearing a costume, consider using a makeup or haircutting cape to keep powder from falling onto the clothing.

TATTOO COVERAGE

Covering tattoos is an essential skill for makeup artists, but it is also an important skill for performers who may have exposed tattoos. Knowing makeup color theory and how concealing works can easily make any tattoo vanish. No matter what the skin tone, the steps that follow will help achieve this illusion.

Step 1: Evaluate

Before starting, identify what main colors comprise the tattoo. Most are blue-green, but many have red, oranges, or an array of colors. When choosing colors for concealing, remember to look to the opposite side of the color wheel for the concealing tone. The following example discusses how to conceal a generic blue-green tattoo.

Step 2: Undertone

According to color theory, orange tones will neutralize blue on the skin. Because tattoos are often blue-green, an orange tone, with a bit of red, is the best concealer choice (see Figure 7.7). This could be a burnt orange or a dusty rose

cream color. Now using the burnt orange tone, apply a consistent layer to the tattoo. This can be a heavy application as the tattoo should be completely covered. Taper the color into the skin tone outside the tattoo area; however, it is not necessary to apply too much undertone to the non-tattoo area.

Step 3: Powder round 1

Using a powder puff, press the puff firmly into the setting powder and then apply firmly onto the skin. It is necessary to press the puff firmly, otherwise the orange will not set properly. Use a liberal amount of powder while dabbing it firmly.

Step 4: Foundation

Using a matching foundation color, apply the cream makeup over the burnt orange undertone

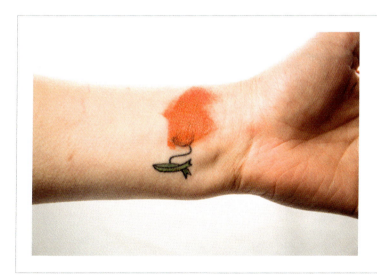

FIGURE 7.7 *Orange tone applied to tattoo.*

Credit: Zeek Creative

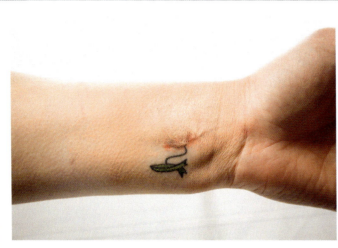

FIGURE 7.8 *Completed tattoo concealment.*

Credit: Zeek Creative

color. Dab a generous amount of product onto the tattoo with a sponge so as not to rub off the undertone makeup. When this step is complete, the tattoo should be completely hidden (see Figure 7.8).

Step 5: Powder round 2

Set the foundation with another heavy coat of powder. If the tattoo is on the arms or neck, consider using a fixer spray to keep the makeup from rubbing off.

CHAPTER 8

EYES AND EYEBROWS

When it comes to creating facial expressions, the eyes are master story tellers. With eyebrows and eyes alone, emotions are conveyed, and stories are told. A little bit of color and contour can change the shape of the eyes, add emphasis, and brighten the face. The possibilities and color combinations are endless. For the stage, the audience needs to see a performer's eyes, often to read his or her expression at a glance.

There are special tricks to working with stage makeup as it relates to the eyes and eyebrows. Everyday makeup may be fine for intimate black-box theatres; however, when a performer steps onto the stage of a thousand seat auditorium, it is imperative that time and attention is given to enhancing the performer's eyes. This chapter discusses different eye and eyebrow products available, as well as several techniques appropriate for the stage.

EYESHADOW

It is easy to get lost when choosing eyeshadow products. There are thousands upon thousands of colors from which to choose, and each seem to react differently. Color is a great thing, but sometimes too much color destroys an effect or draws attention to the wrong feature. Before settling on color, figure out what effect is needed, then work to find the color that tells the story.

To break it down in the simplest terms, eyeshadow is essentially eye contour. The goal is to bring definition to the eyes, shaping them in a desired fashion. This can be done using only shadow and highlight techniques. The fun happens when color is applied. Shaping can still occur, and should for the stage, but the trick is finding the compromise between shaping and color.

Shaping

As discussed later in the book, contour color can be used to change the shape of any feature on the face. The eyes are no exception. Knowing how to change the shape or placement can help when designing makeup applications.

A. **Placement:** Eyeshadow can be used to draw emphasis to certain areas of the eyes and appear to change the natural spacing of the eyes.

- If the eyes are naturally close together, applying highlight color to the lacrimal areas can make the eyes appear further apart (see Figure 8.1). Remember anywhere that highlight is placed will appear to be larger in surface area. Applying a small amount of contour or eyeshadow on the outer edges of the eyes will aid in the illusion that the eyes are spaced normally.

- If the eyes are naturally far apart, applying highlight or light eyeshadow colors to the outer areas of the eyes – while applying contour color or darker tones to the lacrimal areas – will make the eyes appear

FIGURE 8.2 *Highlight applied to the outer eyes to decrease width.*

Credit: Zeek Creative

closer together (see Figure 8.2). Contour color makes the surface appear to recede in space causing the outside of the eyes to look larger.

B. **Manipulation:** Eyeshadow can be used to create folds and wrinkles, and it can change the natural shape of the eye.

- If the eyes are smaller, lighter tones and highlights can be used on the eyelid and lacrimal areas to brighten the eyes. This same technique also applies when the eyes are inset, hooded, or deep set.

- If the eye lid has little to no definition, eyeshadow can be used to create an eye crease effect causing the eye to appear larger and more open (see Figure 8.2). The wider the eyes appear on stage, the easier it is for the audience to see.

- If the eyes are almond shaped, eyeshadow can be used to make them appear more round. By applying contouring in the eye crease in a rounded shape will help widen the natural almond shape. Cutting off the eyeshadow at the outside end will keep the eyes from looking longer.

FIGURE 8.1 *Highlight applied in the lacrimal area to increase width.*

Credit: Zeek Creative

FIGURE 8.3 *Eyeshadow used to create definition.*

Credit: Zeek Creative

- If the eyes are rounder and naturally wide, eyeshadow can be used to make them appear longer. By using contour in the eye crease in a long horizontal shape, pulling it out, and blending away at the outer corner, the eyes will lose much of their roundness and appear narrow.

Color

When choosing eyeshadow colors, there are three things to evaluate – the first is the skin tone, the second is eye color, and the third is production design. Each of these should be given careful consideration before settling on a color palette for the makeup. This is especially true in theatres where performers are required to provide their own makeup and design.

A. **Skin tone:** While almost any color can work on every skin tone, there are some colors that work better with different complexions. For lighter skin tones, pinks and lighter colors work well on stage and in everyday settings. Bright or pale tones can work to reflect the light and make the eyes pop. Light complexions may want to stray from using too many dark tones, which can cause the eyes to look hooded or create a bruising effect. For darker skin tones, bold dark tones work very well and will complement the deep color found in dark complexions (see Figure 8.4). Bright colors will stand out well against bronze and ebony tones; however, light pinks and pale tones can make the skin look dry. Eyeshadows with golden sparkle will keep dark complexions from appearing dry, so warm sparkle can be a valuable asset.

B. **Eye color:** This was touched on in Chapter 4, but it necessitates repeating. Whenever choosing an eyeshadow color, decide if it is important to emphasize the eye color.

FIGURE 8.4 *Bright color on dark skin tone.*

Credit: Zeek Creative

Remember to utilize the color wheel when choosing hues to pop out natural tones. Blue eye colors will pop with orange-rust colors, green eye colors will pop with reds and oranges, and gold flecks stand out with purples. Brown eyes look good with almost any color, but if there are flecks of colors within the iris consider choosing a complementary color for enhancement. These tips are only important if the purpose of the eyeshadow is to emphasize the eyes.

C. **Show design:** For makeup applications where eye color emphasis is not necessary, choose a color that coordinates with the costume or makeup design. Time periods can dictate the color of the eyeshadow no matter what the eye color may be or the skin tone. Also, show design may lend itself to a more creative palette. Determine if the production has specific color requirements before choosing the appropriate eyeshadow color. Often a natural effect is all that is required. For those cases, a neutral palette of earth tones works best.

Application

Now that the shape and placement of the eyes has been established and the color palette has been chosen, the final step is to actually apply the product. There is one key rule to keep in mind when application begins. *Always remember that everything applied to the eyes should help them appear more open.* This is the most important aspect for stage as the eyes convey emotion and show expression. The key to applying color in the form of eyeshadow and still creating bright eyes is to focus on the eyelid and use the makeup as contour, not only as color. These tips for application focus on the feminine corrective use of eyeshadow. As described in Chapter 11, masculine makeup does not utilize eyeshadow color; however, emphasizing the eyes in masculine corrective is just as important as in the feminine corrective application.

When applying basic eyeshadow for stage, it is beneficial to use three different tones: a highlight color, a mid-range color, and a dark color. The dark color is used as the contour tone, and the mid-range helps bridge the gap between the highlight color and the darker color. As stated before, brightening the eyelid helps to create the illusion of a wide eye. Making the eyes appear wide allows the audience to see expressions easier. By placing the highlight color directly onto the eyelid, the eyelid will appear bright and bold. This trick is especially helpful if the eyes are naturally hooded or inset.

After the highlight is applied, then the colors can be added. These colors act as contour so determine where the eye crease should be. Makeup allows for total manipulation of facial features. If the area of the eyes is flatter and there is little definition, eyeshadow can be used to create a crease and shape the eye. Whatever the shape, using a combination of the mid-range color and the dark color can help create subtle contrast from the bright eyelid and add definition. There are many color ranges available. Examples of highlight, mid-range, and dark color combinations are as follows: pale blue to navy, cream to brown, lavender to plum, peach to copper. With many choices, remembering shape, eye color, and design will be helpful in choosing a color for the desired eyeshadow.

EYELINER

If the goal is to make the eyes appear wider on stage, then eyeliner would be the most essential technique in the execution. Whether playing a masculine or feminine character, eyeliner should be a staple of a performer's repertoire.

Products

Before application, the right product for the production must be chosen. Knowing which eyeliner medium to use can be overwhelming, and there are pros and cons to each one. Following are the types of eyeliners most popular for stage performer use.

A. **Cake liner:** Cake liner is also called pan-cake makeup. Just like with foundation pan-cake makeup, cake liner comes as a dry product. When water is added, it turns into a liquid and reacts just like paint. Cake liner is easy to use, very versatile, and should be applied with a thin brush or tapered eyeliner brush. Because it is water-based, cake liner is susceptible to perspiration and can easily run.

B. **Gel liner:** Gel liner is an eyeliner product with a thick consistency. Due to the consistency, gel eyeliners usually come in small glass pots and are easy to scoop out using a makeup spatula. Angled eyeliner brushes are the best tools for application as the thin angle helps plant the thick product evenly over the lash line. Gel liner is often water-proof making it useful for performers who perspire heavily. This also makes it difficult to remove after performances and requires stronger makeup remover products.

C. **Felt-tipped liquid liner:** Another form of liquid liner is the kind that is already in liquid form. These usually come with a small tapered brush for easy application. The felt tip adds precision just like a makeup brush for the cake liner. The felt-tipped applicator makes liquid liners easy to manipulate and very versatile. Pre-mixed liquid liners can also be found in water-proof brands making them a nice alternative to cake liner. The downside is that because of sanitation concerns with the applicator, the eyeliner container should only be used on one performer and then discarded once the production is complete.

D. **Pencil liner:** Eyeliner pencils are the most cost-effective eyeliner product. They are often a waxy or soft consistency for easy application. Mostly oil based, they do not run with perspiration and tears. Pencil liners are easy to control along the lash line; however, creating smooth wings and tips can be challenging. Pencils should be continually sharpened to ensure the end is pointed for better precision. If the desired effect is an intense, diffused line, pencil liners would be very effective. They also come in a variety of colors, unlike with the other eyeliner mediums. Even white pencil liners can be used inside the eyelash line on the waterline, to make the eyes appear even bigger.

Application

To achieve the widest eyes possible, a couple tricks can be done to enhance the illusion. The first is in the spacing of the eyeliner. Typically for daily eyeliner use, the line is placed right onto the eyelash line whether on the top or the bottom eyelash line. This is followed by mascara to join the colors together. For stage, because the eye makeup is meant for people sitting 10, 20, or 50 feet away applying eyeliner so close to the lash line is not necessary. Often for larger theatres, drawing the eyeliner line beside the eyelash line is acceptable. This increases the white area around the iris causing the eyes to appear wider. Follow this effect up with a white eyeliner pencil on the lower waterline and the wide-eye effect becomes very noticeable.

The second trick is to not connect the upper and lower eyeliner lines. This thought is counter-cultural to daily makeup use, but effective for stage. When drawing the upper and lower eyeliner lines, start in the lacrimal region and pull the line toward the outside edge. Draw the line until reaching the outer corner, then finish off with an eyeliner wing. With the bottom line, stop the applicator about a quarter of an inch from the upper line. Applying a small amount of highlight between the two lines will make the distance appear even further. Eyeliner drawn completely

FIGURE 8.5 *Eyeliner spacing in the corner of the eyes.*
Credit: Zeek Creative

around the eyes cuts off the eyes from the rest of the face. By leaving the end open, the audience is tricked into believing the eye continues outward.

EYEBROWS

There is a saying about eyebrows that many have heard: *Eyebrows are sisters, not twins*. While this old adage may be true for daily wear, it is not true for the stage. When a performer walks on stage, the audience scrutinizes the character. Everything about the performer should be executed for a reason. If the eyebrows are perfect, then that says something about the character; if the eyebrows are askew, that says something different. Neither masculine or feminine performers are exempt from eyebrow upkeep. Makeup on the eyebrows serves two purposes. It helps to unify the brow hair, and makeup helps create shape. Before discussing these techniques, it helps to know what makeup products are available for use.

Products

There are four main eyebrow products available. Evaluate what effect and shape are needed for the production before settling on a medium. Each one has positive and negative points.

A. **Eyebrow pencil:** Pencils are the easiest product to use when filling in and shaping brow hair (see Figure 8.6). By keeping the point parallel to the face, the hair can be colored without the tip touching the skin. With a sharpened point, however, a very dark eyebrow color can be achieved. Unfortunately, it can be difficult to achieve crisp edges with a

FIGURE 8.6 *Eyebrow pencil used on the eyebrows.*

Credit: Zeek Creative

brow pencil point. Eyebrow pencils are best for brows that need to be darkened but do not necessarily need a defined shape.

B. **Powder:** Powder offers the greatest variety of colors (see Figure 8.7). Performers do not need to only use specific eyebrow powders; eyeshadow colors also work well to darken and shape brows. Eyebrow brushes with stiffer bristles help control the product, and it is easier to define the shape when using a brush. Intense color may be more difficult to achieve, however, and smudging can occur more

frequently if the eyebrow is touched during a performance.

C. **Cake liner:** For bold eyebrows with intense color, wet mediums are the product of choice. Cake liner is the water-based product that comes as a pressed powder and requires water to activate (see Figure 8.8). This offers high versatility and can easily create whatever shape desired. A thin brush can draw on individual hairs and create realism in the details. Because it is water-based, heavy perspiration can cause cake liner to run and smudge.

D. **Gel/pomade:** Much like with gel eyeliner, eyebrow gels and pomades are tinted products used to help control brow hair and color the skin (see Figure 8.9). They are a thicker consistency than the other products and are often water-resistant. A thin brush can help create detailed, individually drawn hairs, and clean edges are easy to obtain. Because of its consistency, the makeup can be difficult to remove if a mistake is made in the application. Using eyebrow stencils can help create nice shapes using gel and pomade.

FIGURE 8.7 *Powder used on the eyebrows.*

Credit: Zeek Creative

FIGURE 8.8 *Cake liner used on the eyebrows.*

Credit: Zeek Creative

FIGURE 8.9 *Gel liner used on the eyebrows.*

Credit: Zeek Creative

Color

Choosing a color for the eyebrows should not be difficult. It is best to remember when matching colors to use a product that is the natural color of the brows or is a shade or two darker. This is especially true for performers with fair skin and hair who often have very light eyebrows. On stage, it is very easy for eyebrows to blend in with the skin tone no matter what the complexion. That is why grooming the eyebrows with a color a shade darker is important. This is as true for masculine performers as it is for feminine performers. A bold, natural brow works to everyone's benefit.

Application

Whether for feminine or masculine performers, the same rules for applying eyebrow makeup apply to both. The first rule is no matter what shape is chosen, the brows should still look natural. It is easy to get carried away with eyebrow shapes. Performers with naturally thick eyebrows have a tendency to apply heavy makeup to the brows making them look larger. Performers with very thin eyebrows tend to want to keep their brows thin, forgetting that the eyebrows still need to be visible from the back row of the audience. Remember that eyebrow makeup is about unifying the hairs and shaping the brows with a little color while keeping them natural.

The second rule to remember is that the eyebrows should still be used to make the eyes appear wider. Adding an arch or cheating the brows higher opens the space above the eyelid brightening the eye area. If the eyebrows are drawn heavy and thick, they detract from the eyes and can make the brow bone appear darker – the opposite of the bright effect desired. Clearly not every character in the theatrical world needs bright, wide eyes; however, large theatre spaces translate performer's features better when performers' eyes are visible.

The last rule to consider is expression. When drawing an effective eyebrow shape, keep these points in mind:

- If the eyebrows are drawn too deep at the inside line, the performer can look intense.
- If the eyebrows are drawn very pointed in the middle, the performer will look angry.
- If the eyebrows are drawn too high in an extreme arch, the performer will look surprised.
- If the eyebrows are drawn too small, the performer's face will look larger.
- If the ends of the eyebrows are dragged too low, they will cut off the eyes and make the performer look sad.
- If the eyebrows are drawn too large, the performer can look crazy.

CHAPTER 9

LIPS

Many audience members may say, *if I can't see the actor's mouth, then I can't hear them.* Whether this is a statement born from a psychological perception or merely personal preference is yet to be determined. Whichever the case, the lips are vitally important to the look of a performer, and care must be given so the audience can see them. No matter if the character is masculine or feminine, the lips can easily be obscured by lighting and overshadowed by hair and costumes. At other times, just emphasizing lips will not be enough. Perhaps there is a time-period specific show that requires reshaping the lips, or a show where they appear to be gone altogether. It is these effects and more that make discussing lips so important. When talking about lips, there are two aspects that need defining. The first is the lipliner, and the second is the lip color.

LIPLINER

Lipliner is often misunderstood by everyone (see Figure 9.1). Individuals, on a daily basis, do not see the need for it, and performers do not give it value. It is unfortunate that lipliner does not get its due because it will enhance most any look, and it fulfills three very important purposes.

The first and most important of the three is that lipliner keeps the lip color from bleeding onto the skin. Because liners are waxy and a thicker consistency than most lip colors, the liner pencil creates a barrier around the lips that keeps color in. Without liner, lip colors will soften around the lip edges causing them to smear outside the lip shape. The color starts to spread away from the lips and will require continual touch-ups. With a lipliner, the bleeding effect is stopped, and the color is contained

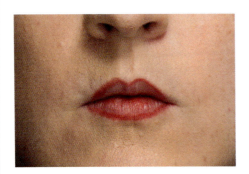

FIGURE 9.1 *Lipliner used around lip perimeter.*

Credit: Zeek Creative

FIGURE 9.2 *Lip color blended into lipliner.*

Credit: Zeek Creative

only inside the area outlined by the liner. For the performer who is on stage for most of the show, this feature is important. The heat from the lights and the performer's own body heat can easily cause lip colors to run, an effect that can be controlled using lipliner.

Second, lipliner helps define the shape of the lips. Asymmetrical lip shapes are quite common. Lipliner can be used to correct these shapes, making them more uniform. With a lipliner, new shapes can be drawn over and around the natural lips. Larger lips can be drawn smaller, and smaller lips can be over-drawn. Liners make it easier to manipulate shapes than just using lip color.

Last, blending with lipliner can help create contour eliminated by lighting (see Figure 9.2). It has already been stated that lighting washes out the natural features of the performer. The lips are no exception. By using lipliner and blending it into the lip color, two-tone contouring effects can be created. These blending techniques that

simulate contour help define the lips, giving them emphasis with applied highlights and shadow.

LIP PRODUCT

When discussing lips, using the term lip color is more accurate than saying lipstick. Makeup should be viewed as a collection of products and colors to be used as the individual sees fit. For the lips, certainly lipstick can be used, but other products can be used as well. Cream stage makeup colors, for instance, can be used just like using lipliner pencils or colorful eyeliner pencils. It is all in how they are used. If there is a color that works for the overall makeup, then there is generally a way to make that product work. When performers can get away from the stigma that products have to be used for only their original intent – i.e. lipstick for lips, eyeshadow for eyes – then true creativity can begin.

Finishes

There are two finishes of lip colors: glossy and matte. Glossy colors tend to have a sheen to them and can often be described as dewy (see Figure 9.3). The lips will look moist and may even glisten with a glossy color. Often for stage, mature feminine performers will wear glossy lip colors as this helps add a freshness to their character. Matte finishes do not have a shine to them (see Figure 9.3). If cream makeup is used as a lip color, then the lips will have a matte finish. Matte colors have little shine to them, but they make up for this with their bold colors. Mature feminine performers should refrain from wearing matte colors as this will make the lips look dryer and parched. Young ingénue roles can use either matte or glossy lip colors. Ultimately, one finish is not better than the other; the role and age of the performer should be taken into account before a lip product is chosen.

FIGURE 9.4 *Matte finish.*

Credit: Zeek Creative

Color

This topic was touched on in Chapter 4 when discussing color theory and its relation to lip and skin color. Before picking out a color for the lips, evaluate the skin tone and the production design. Lighter skin tones look best with light pinks and reds for lip colors. Warmer tones will help to freshen the face while cool pinks can make the skin look paler on pale complexions. Darker skin tones do well with deeper reds, burgundies, and purples. Pale lip colors such as pinks and cool tones can make the lips appear dry. Products with intrinsic shimmer will counter the effect of dry skin. Gold shimmer works better and is perceived as healthier and fresher than silver shimmer. Warm lip color tones add a brighter glow to the face. If the production calls for a historical lip color, concede to the design rather than normal lip conventions.

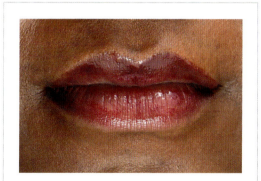

FIGURE 9.3 *Glossy finish.*

Credit: Zeek Creative

LIP EFFECTS

Effect #1: Over-Drawing

Sometimes a performer may have an upper lip or lower lip that is small in size, or maybe the show is designed in a period or culture where lips need to be a larger shape than the performer has naturally. Over-drawing is a technique where the lipliner and lip color are taken past the natural lip shape (see Figure 9.5). This is easily achieved by starting with a lipliner and drawing the desired shape outside the natural lip. It may be that only the bottom lip needs to be over-drawn, or it could only be the top lip. Whichever one it is, once the liner is applied, lip color can be added inside the lined area. Often the lip color will be added onto the skin rather than just onto the lips.

Effect #2: Under-Drawing

Sometimes a performer may have an upper lip or lower lip that is large in size, or maybe the

FIGURE 9.5 *Example of over-drawing lips.*

Credit: Zeek Creative

FIGURE 9.6 *Example of under-drawing lips.*

Credit: Zeek Creative

show is designed in a period or culture where lips need to be a smaller shape than the performer has naturally. Under-drawing is the opposite to over-drawing where the lipliner and lip color are applied inside the natural lip shape. Lipliner comes in handy once again to trace the desired shape inside the performer's own lip shape. Often this may only be done on the edges to create a curved effect, or it could be to define the top lip peaks. Whatever the reason, once the lipliner color is applied, lip color is applied inside the traced line. Since the natural lip color is still seen around the edges, using foundation or highlight color is the last step to under-drawing the lips. Using foundation or highlight will not only help conceal the lip color, it will also brighten the lip area and cause the mouth to appear youthful.

Effect #3: Concealing

Creating fantasy creatures without lips can be fun. There may not be many instances where

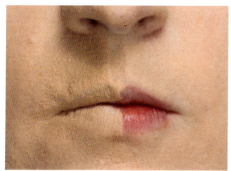

FIGURE 9.7 *Example of concealing lips.*

Credit: Zeek Creative

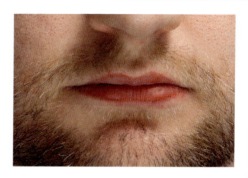

FIGURE 9.8 *Example of masculine lip definition.*

Credit: Zeek Creative

concealing the lips will be necessary; however, it is a useful trick to know. It is not very difficult to do – especially knowing color theory and how to conceal various colors (see Figure 9.7). First, evaluate the color of the lips. Most often lips are pink, red, or a warm tan color. Cool colors, greens and blues, will neutralize pinks and reds. Second, dabbing a light application of green over the lips will neutralized the color. After a layer of powder, foundation can be applied, and the lips will vanish. Because they are three-dimensional objects, lips may still have slight shadows around them. This depends on the natural curve of the lips.

Effect #4: Masculine Lips

Most of the effects already listed deal with feminine lip preparations. As will be described in Chapter 11, masculine characters do not require lips that are full and dynamic. The purpose of lip color for them is merely to define the shape of the lips without enhancing the color (see Figure 9.8). Often performers' mouths surrounded with facial hair can get lost if they are not defined. This is a simple technique of applying a lipliner color to the edges of the lips, then using a clear lip balm or gloss to blend the color inward. It is an easy effect, but it makes a difference.

CHAPTER 10

BONE STRUCTURE MAKEUP

In the simplest terms, the human face consists of nothing but ridges and valleys, high points and low points. Exploring facial dimensions is the key feature to this application, making it the building block for all other projects to follow. The importance does not come through complexity but through anatomical understanding of skeletal patterns.

The goal for this makeup is to define and chisel the facial features, creating a sunken, hollow face. By merging the idea of emaciation with the structure of a skeleton, this makeup will look like a skull-with-skin application. Before getting started, use fingertips to explore key areas of the face and identify the anatomical features listed in Chapter 3.

Step 1: Apply foundation

- Choose a foundation color that matches the natural skin tone or is a shade or two lighter. Try not to choose a tone that is too white, or the highlight color may not stand out.

- Use a sponge to apply foundation to the face while blending it down past the jawline. Also apply a layer onto the eyelids.

- Apply translucent powder with a powder puff to set the makeup. Press the powder puff into the powder, shake the excess powder from the puff, and firmly blot each area where foundation was applied.

Step 2: Apply contour

As discussed in Chapter 5, contour is essential to stage makeup and bone structure makeup is no exception. Contour color will be used to slim the face and will be applied most anywhere there is a natural recession in the face.

- Start by choosing a color such as dark brown, ebony, cinnamon or another color in that tonal family. Most theatrical makeup kits will have a pre-designated contour color. When applying the color, only use a light application. It is easy to increase intensity with cream makeup, so it is best to start light and go darker.

• Apply contour color to the following places: brow bones, temples, cheekbones, jawline, chin, nose, and eye sockets.

A. **Brow bones**: Finding this bone can be tricky. Start by using fingertips and exploring the Frontalis bone. Most people will have slight indentions up toward the hairline above the eyebrows. To slim the forehead, lightly plant contour color in this groove. The bone should resemble a curved "L". Blend the color inward toward the center of the forehead while softening the line toward the hairline. Softening does not mean blending. Softening creates a fuzzy application of intense color. The color should not be heavy as it only suggests the presence on an indentation (see Figure 10.1).

B. **Temples**: The temples are the natural indention between the eyes and the hairline. Apply color into this recess, blend it back toward the hairline, then lightly soften the line on the opposite side of the contour color. When this is complete, the brow bone will seem very prominent (see Figure 10.2).

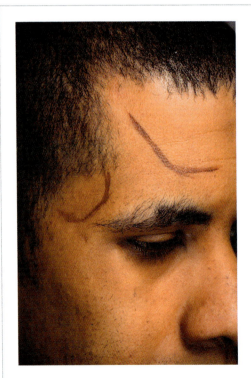

FIGURE 10.1 *Brow bone and temple placement.*

Credit: Zeek Creative

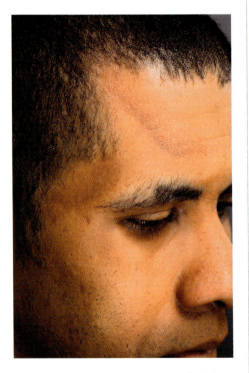

FIGURE 10.2 *Brow bone and temple blended.*

Credit: Zeek Creative

C. **Cheekbones**: Start by pinpointing the highest point of the Zygomatic bone, the cheek's apple. Plant a line of color starting at mid-ear and brush it under the apple toward the nose. Make sure not to connect this line with the nose but stop an inch or two short. This should be a gently sloping curve. Next, create a "y" shape by adding a small blended stick curving down toward your jawline. This line follows the indention created when the Masseter drops away toward the teeth. Now blend the long stick up and blend the small stick back. Be sure to soften the lines on the opposite side. This contouring gives the illusion that the cheek is sunken and withered (see Figures 10.3 and 10.4).

D. **Jawline**: Find the point of the jawbone just below the earlobes. Apply contour color under the jaw and around toward the chin. Plant the contour color first; then blend it down toward the neck while softening it up toward the face. Using a makeup sponge to blend this contour may be easier than using a brush.

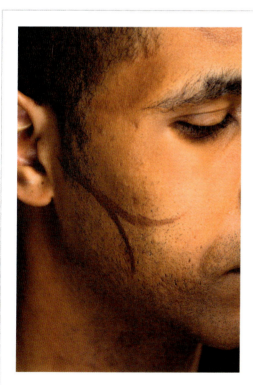

FIGURE 10.3 *Cheek contour placement.*

Credit: Zeek Creative

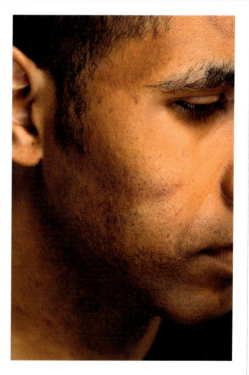

FIGURE 10.4 *Cheek contour blended.*

Credit: Zeek Creative

E. **Chin**: Emphasize the chin by adding a small downward curve of contour color between the lower lip and the ball of the chin. This merely helps to create definition, so lightly fade this line out. It should not be bold or dark but a suggestion of the natural indention.

F. **Nose**: If this application were going to mimic a real skull, the nose would not exist since it is decomposable cartilage and not bone; however, for the purpose of this makeup and as an applicable convention, this makeup will make the nose look angular and bony. On the side of the nose, use a brush to create a "V" or arrow shape down at the nostril. Then lightly blend the color toward the cheek and up toward the brow. Soften the line next to the bridge of the nose.

G. **Eye sockets**: To create a living skull, the eyes will be blocked out entirely to form deep eye sockets (see Figure 10.5). Use fingertips to locate the natural eye socket bones – that area when firm bone falls away into the fleshy eye. Start by planting color in an oval shape right inside the fleshy part of the socket. The line around the eye should be the darkest contour of the whole makeup. Next, blend this line onto the eyelid, filling in the entire socket with color. Once the area is filled, soften the outer line blending slightly with the foundation color. This is called blended intensity. Over-blending will create raccoon-eyes; keep the color concentrated to the edges and softened where the bone meets the fleshy eye. It should look as if the light is hitting the cheekbone before falling away into shadow.

FIGURE 10.5 *Blended eye socket contour.*

Credit: Zeek Creative

Once all contouring has been applied, powder everything. This allows colors to blend together without moving the under-layers too much.

Step 3: Apply highlights

- Each time low points on the face are emphasized, the high points must be emphasized as well. This contrast of contour and highlight is very important as it increases the natural dimensions of the face.

- Highlight will be applied everywhere contour was applied. Chose a color that is several tones lighter than the foundation color. Most theatrical makeup kits have a highlight color designated; however, mixing the highlight color is very common.

- Highlight will be applied to the following places: brow bones, cheekbones, jawline, chin, nose, and eye sockets (see Figure 10.6).

  A. **Brow bones**: The brow and temple contours reveal the apex of the brow bone. Place a line of highlight color along the middle ridge where the bone would be naturally higher. Blend the highlight out toward these two contour areas while not blending it directly next to the contour. The contour may need to be softened into the highlight to round out the bone. Just remember, no harsh lines.

  B. **Cheekbones**: Now that you know where the Zygomatic peak is located, place highlight color there and blend it down toward the cheek and toward the nose. This is a soft application and is never bold.

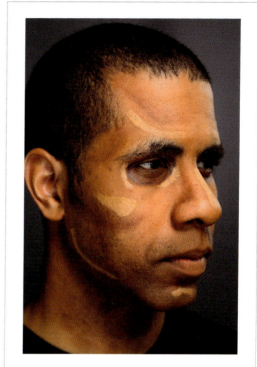

FIGURE 10.6 *Highlight marking.*
Credit: Zeek Creative

  C. **Jawline**: Find the jawline points again and apply highlight color to the area. Blend the color along the Mandible edge but keep it concentrated to the jawline (see Figure 10.7). This area is also located under the "y" contour of the cheek. Jawline highlight is very effective in making the face appear square and bony.

  D. **Chin**: Apply a light application of highlight to the ball of the chin and blend it outward.

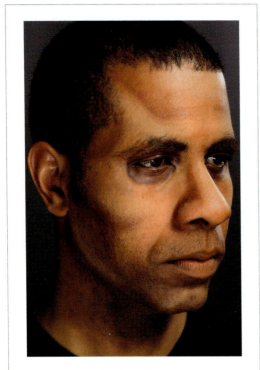

FIGURE 10.7 *Blended highlights.*

Credit: Zeek Creative

E. **Nose**: Apply a line of highlight on the nose bridge between the two contour arrows and soften the color into those contours. Once blended, this will make the nose appear long and lean.

F. **Eye sockets**: Using highlight, plant color along the outer edge of the eye socket and the inner edge of the eye socket. This makes the eye look as if it is enclosed in parentheses. Now lightly blend these highlights out toward the temple/cheek area and the lacrimal/nose area while lightly softening the highlight into the

socket contour color. Again, the makeup should give the effect that the light is hitting the bone before abruptly falling away into darkness.

Now that the highlights are complete, powder these areas as before. This sets the makeup for the final step.

Step 4: Extra

- There are several techniques that can take this makeup from good to great. Adding pockets of intensity and moments of interest help create believable characters who truly come alive.

- An eyeliner or eyebrow pencil can be used to add intense color. The best colors to use are either dark brown or black depending on your skin tone.

- Moments of intense highlight can also help to draw attention to bony aspects of the face.

   A. Determine where the deepest shadows would be in the makeup. These are the points that would be the darkest crevices or the most recessed places in a natural skull such as the following: crook of the brow bone, edge of the temple, lower crook of the cheek contour, beside the nostril, and outer and inner edges of the eye sockets.

   B. Using a makeup pencil, draw a small mark in each of these areas (see Figure 10.8). Only draw one line of color in these areas because too much color will destroy the work.

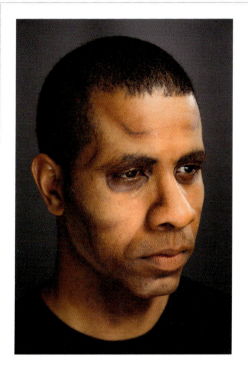

FIGURE 10.8 *Added Intensity.*

Credit: Zeek Creative

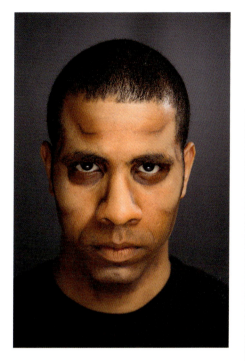

FIGURE 10.9 *Completed application.*

Credit: Zeek Creative

C. Using a contour brush, soften these lines along the contour edge that has already been established. Make sure they transition into the colors well. Blend them into the highlight or foundation color to make them softer if needed. The deepening color helps define the contour while emphasizing the dramatic shadows.

D. Go back to the highlight color. Determine where the highest points on the face are located. Using a brush, apply small points of intensity to these spots. Areas could include: brow ridges, outer and inner eye socket corners, and jawline (see Figure 10.9).

CHAPTER 11

CORRECTIVE MAKEUP

The term *corrective* can be deceptive. To say *corrective* implies that a feature or characteristic needs to be fixed. For stage, the term refers to making facial features more symmetrical and emphasizing those features. The two applications in this chapter are considered the basic stage makeup of a performer. Its purpose goes beyond beauty makeup. Corrective techniques utilize highlight and shadow to shape the face once the stage lights wash out the features. Also, facial focal points must be emphasized so audience members can distinguish characters and expressions.

Once a performer steps onto the stage, the audience subconsciously tries to make one determination – Is the character male or female? This is the challenge of corrective makeup. No matter the gender of the performer, it is often important to make obvious the character's gender. Male characters typically can appear strong and confident especially if they are leads in musicals or operas. To achieve this construct

of masculinity, the techniques convey sharp angles and bold features to define the face. For feminine characters, rounder shapes sporting soft curves and dynamic colors are the defining features. When gender-swapping in a production, performers should remember these differences in masculine and feminine makeups. The easiest way for an actress to play a convincing masculine role is to utilize masculine corrective techniques. The same can be said for an actor playing feminine roles. Corrective makeup goes beyond a performer's gender and identity; it concerns the character and how the director wants them portrayed.

This chapter breaks down the two types of corrective makeups and gives a step-by-step description on creating each one. Decide which one works for the performer and follow those steps. Remember, the bigger the theatre space the stronger the highlights and shadow colors. This is true for both corrective applications.

MASCULINE CORRECTIVE MAKEUP

There are several points to remember when applying masculine corrective. The first is that the majority of men do not wear makeup as a daily routine. For this reason, the audience does not generally expect male characters to look like they are wearing makeup. Maintaining this expectation is a very important goal for masculine corrective makeup. The size of the theatre space should always be evaluated before applying a masculine corrective makeup because the bigger the house the heavier the makeup. The following techniques work for all house sizes; it is only the intensity that would change. Just as in bone structure, it is makeup's job to add the contouring back into the face when features are washed away by lighting. Intended male characters should most often not look *made-up* but should look like themselves on a theatrical stage.

The second point to remember is, most often, male characters should look masculine. It is easy to think that makeup makes everyone look feminine, but that is only because of poor execution. As long as masculine features are kept chiseled and rugged then any performer will look masculine on stage.

Step 1: Apply foundation

- Apply a thin layer of foundation over the skin and down onto the neck. Spotlights can wash out three-dimensional features and make faces appear pale. To counter this effect, it is acceptable for masculine foundation colors to be a shade or two darker than the actual skin tone. The darker shade will work to create a rugged appearance for male characters. Choosing a pale foundation will make a character look more feminine and the spotlight will wash out the features. Now use a powder puff to apply setting powder to the face by firmly blotting the foundation color.

Step 2: Apply contour

- Apply contour subtly; stage makeup is more effective for shadows to look natural. If contours become too heavy, the face will look skeletal and stylized. Again, this depends on the size of the theatrical space.

- Apply contour in the following locations: brow bones, temples, cheekbones, jawbone, chin, nose, and lacrimal areas.

  A. **Brow bones**: Refer to the brow bone contour application in Chapter 10. This application is very similar. Emphasizing the brow bone gives the illusion of a strong, angular forehead. To slim the forehead, lightly plant contour color in the bone groove. The bone should resemble a curved "L." Blend the color inward toward the center of the forehead while softening the line toward the hairline. Remember, softening creates a fuzzy application of intense color; however, the color for this makeup should not be heavy as it only suggests the presence on the indention.

  B. **Temples**: Determine whether the contour line for the temple region should be circular or square. Use fingertips to determine which shape naturally occurs. Now place a line of contour color outlining this area and blend it back toward the hairline. Be sure to soften the line next to the brow bone. This is another light application only to denote an angular face structure and to set masculine features apart from feminine features.

C. **Cheekbones**: Emphasize the cheekbones to create the illusion that they are chiseled. Strong, angular cheekbones are the goal. As with each of these masculine effects, choose an intensity that complements the space, so the makeup appears natural.

- Start at the middle of the ear and apply contour color in a curved right angle under the cheekbone and down toward the jawline where the teeth and the Masseter meet. This blending is similar to the cheek contour in the bone structure application except the top arm of the "y" is left off. Do not take the blended line all the way to the jawline but stop it about two inches from the jaw (see Figure 11.1).

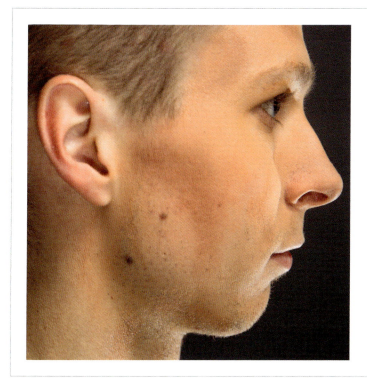

FIGURE 11.1 *Blended cheekbone contour.*

Credit: Zeek Creative

- Blend the top of the curve up. The effect should cup the apple of the cheek while the bottom of the curve gets blended back toward the jawbone. Soften these areas on the opposite sides to eliminate harsh lines.

D. **Jawbone**: Masculine features tend to include strong, square jaw lines, and contour color can be used to emphasize the strong point below the ear. Apply color under the jawline and blend down onto the neck while softening it toward the face. Blend this area well as it is difficult to see if harsh lines linger. Using a sponge to blend is a nice trick for even coverage.

E. **Chin**: Strong, masculine lead characters look best with strong chins. Emphasize the chin by adding a small downward curve of contour color between the lower lip and the ball of the chin. This helps to create definition, so lightly fade this line out. It should not be bold or dark but a suggestion of the natural indention. Apply contour directly under the lower lip and blend it down at the sides. It almost looks like a sideways "C," but it is just a shadow and not defined.

F. **Nose**: Many performers do not need help defining their noses. Adding contour to an already defined nose will only make the nose appear more prominent. If the desire is to make the nose look more angular; however, apply a small

amount of contour on either side of the dorsum. Blend this down toward the face and soften it at the dorsum ridge. This is similar to the nose contour from the bone structure application, except a defined arrow is not needed for masculine corrective.

G. **Lacrimal areas**: The goal for this effect is two-fold. With makeup, a masculine application can not only be angular and strong, but be expressive as well. Often masculine characters are intense on stage. Makeup can help to give characters intense focus just with a little contour in the lacrimal areas. Remember though, masculine characters are not supposed to look like they are wearing makeup, so subtlety is key.

- Start by placing a small amount of contour color in the lacrimal area of the eye (see Figure 11.2). This can be the strongest contour tone in this entire makeup. Once the color is applied, soften the tone by blending the color down slightly toward the nose and fading it out before reaching halfway down the nose.

- Blend the top area under the eyebrow and above the eyelid. The color should move underneath the natural ridge but above the eye crease. Do not take the contour all the way to the outside eye edge. Blend it from the lacrimal region and allow it to fade away. This contour

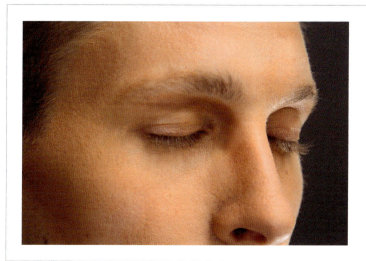

FIGURE 11.2 *Lacrimal contour.*

Credit: Zeek Creative

shadow draws distinction between feminine eyeshadow by making it appear as a natural shadow for men.

Use translucent facial powder, along with a powder puff, to set the makeup now that all the contour color has been applied.

Step 3: Apply highlights

- Apply highlight color beside all the contour points. Choose a highlight color that complements the foundation but is lighter by several tones. Keep in mind that no matter how pale the complexion, plain white should never be used as a highlight color. Consider mixing in foundation, adding white if needed. For darker skin tones make sure to use a golden tone in the highlight. Going too light in the highlight color can make darker tones

appear dry. Test the colors on the neck or jaw before settling on a highlight color. It may be helpful to write the color down on a makeup chart for future reference.

- Apply highlight color to the following areas: brow bones, cheekbones, jawbone, chin, and eyes (see Figure 11.3).

  A. **Brow bones**: The brow and temple contours reveal the apex of the brow bone. Place a line of highlight color along the middle ridge where the bone would naturally be higher. Blend the highlight out toward these two contour areas while not blending it directly next to the contour. Do not forget to soften the contour into the highlight to round out the bone.

  B. **Cheekbones**: Only a small amount of highlight is needed on these areas. Apply

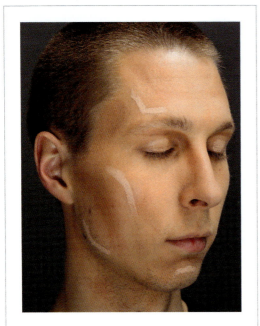

FIGURE 11.3 *Highlight marking.*

Credit: Zeek Creative

a small amount of color above the cheek contour, on the apple of the cheekbones. Once it has been applied, blend it out in all directions.

C. **Jawbone**: Complement the square contour that was applied to the jawline with highlight. Apply a small amount onto the square point of the jaw, making a shape that resembles an "L." Blend it out in all directions until soft. Like most other highlights the jawbone highlight is supposed to resemble a light wash of color.

D. **Chin**: Apply highlight to the ball of the chin and blend it out if the chin needs to appear larger. Taking the highlight down

further and slightly under the chin will also help with the illusion of having a large chin.

E. **Eyes**: Eye makeup is tricky for masculine characters. Too much and they can look feminine, but too little and the eyes get lost. The goal for eye highlight is to emphasize the eyes without conveying a makeup-eyeshadow effect. The eyes should still be bright and expressive though. Apply highlight to the eyelids and blend it up into the eyelid crease. The tone should be subtle and not too bold. Soften the highlight into the shadow color above the crease until they blend together.

After applying the highlights, use the translucent powder and a powder puff to set the makeup.

Step 4: Apply eyeliner

Eyeliner is important even for masculine characters; however, there must be a distinction made from feminine characters. If there is one makeup technique that can make a masculine character look feminine, it is eyeliner. The trick is to keep it subtle, allowing a natural shadow to emerge and not the bold line of color.

• Evaluate the hair and skin tone first. Individuals with fair hair or mid-range browns should consider using a brown or dark brown eyeliner color. For darker skin tones, dark brown tones or black works well. Matching the tone of eyeliner to the color of the hair is a good place to start. A pencil eyeliner is the best product for masculine characters. The line applied by the pencil is usually not bold or sharp but more diffused. This gives the suggestion of shadow around the eye instead of the stark line of a brush.

- Draw a soft line, beginning at the inner eye near the lacrimal area, with the flat of the pencil along the top lash line (see Figure 11.4). Be sure not take the line further than the lashes on the outside, and do not add a *wing* effect to the outside.

- Use one of these two techniques for the bottom lash line: The first is to take contour color and a brush and apply a smudged line to the bottom lash line. Stop this soft line where the lashes end on the outside and inside lash line. The second technique requires using the eyeliner pencil. Lightly draw a series of 4 or 5 dots along the lower lashes in the lash line (see Figure 11.5). This little trick gives the appearance of bold lower lashes without drawing a stark line on the bottom.

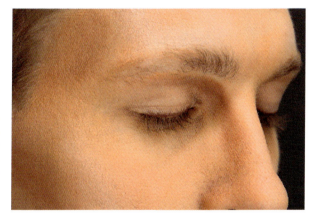

FIGURE 11.4 *Upper eyeliner.*
Credit: Zeek Creative

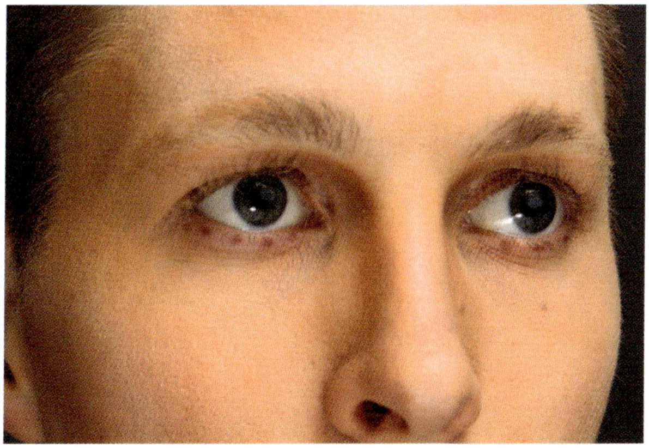

FIGURE 11.5 *Lower eyeliner dots.*
Credit: Zeek Creative

FIGURE 11.6 *Applying eyebrow color.*

Credit: Zeek Creative

Step 5: Eyebrows

It is often a misconception that masculine characters do not need makeup on their eyebrows, but this is not true. Most all performers need makeup on their brows. For gender swapped characters, it is even more essential. Adding color to the eyebrows not only darkens the brow, making them appear thicker and more intense, but it also unifies the brow making them more cohesive. This is necessary for the stage as the eyes convey emotions from the performer.

- Start by choosing a color that matches the hair tone or is slightly darker. For masculine corrective, it is as simple as using an eyebrow or eyeliner pencil. With the side of the pencil tip, back comb the color onto the hair from the inner edge to outer corner (see Figure 11.6). To define the shape a bit, darken the point or the outside end depending on the desired shape. Masculine characters typically have strong, angular brows so bold shapes work best. Be sure to keep the shape natural, however; geometric shapes are not the goal.

- Brush the brows with the tip of the pencil following the growth pattern of the hair. This step adds the shape to the brow as the previous step added the color. Try to keep the brows natural, refraining from making them solid.

Step 6: Blush

Blush is not just for feminine characters, but it is an essential part of masculine corrective.

FIGURE 11.7 *Blush application.*

Credit: Zeek Creative

Foundation was already used to even out the skin tone and unify undertones. The purpose of blush is to add color and life back into the face. Masculine characters have a wide array of colors to choose from since the goal is to make them look ruddy. Burnt reds, burnt oranges, and even deep pinks are nice tones to use. In some situations, a sunburn effect is perfectly acceptable for masculine characters.

- First, decide how the character is supposed to look. Do they like to be outdoors, or do they work inside often? If the character's face was flushed, that is the tone to use. If the skin tone is fair, stray away from dark tones like Chestnut and Raisin. For darker skin tones, brighter reds and oranges are very effective.

- Next, use a blush brush and saturate it with color. Knock excess powder off the brush, then lightly apply it into the contour color. Start in the cheek area and bring the color onto the Zygomatic bone. Be sure it is not too intense though. Once these areas are done, move onto the temples, forehead, and jawline.

- Think of blush as not only adding life but acting as a bridge between highlight and contour. Allow the color to blend the light and dark areas of the face. Be sure not to over use the color – keep it subtle.

Step 7: Lips

Unless it is for a specific character, masculine characters should not look as if they are wearing lipstick on stage. The problem with most individuals is that their lips can be thin, unformed, or fade into the skin tone. What is needed is not lip color but lip definition. This is easy to achieve using only a lip pencil and a dab of lip balm.

- Using a lip pencil that matches the lip color, take the tip and lightly define the edges. Pay attention to the peaks and bottom lip. Lightly lining them only adds definition and corrects any inconsistencies in the lips, so this is a subtle color application. Consider using the side of the pencil tip to plant a light application onto the lips.

- Applying lip balm is a nice finishing touch for masculine lips. Use a brush to apply a light amount. The brush will help blend the lip

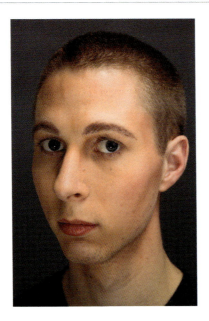

FIGURE 11.8 *Completed application.*

Credit: Zeek Creative

pencil color around and soften the lines made with the point of the pencil, while adding a dampness to the lips that will leave them looking fresh and healthy (see Figure 11.8).

FEMININE CORRECTIVE MAKEUP

Feminine corrective adheres to the same expectations as the masculine corrective application. Contour must be used to add the shadows back into the face, so the audience can see the performer's expressions. Always note the size of the theatre before applying this basic stage makeup. The intensity will change given the house size; however, feminine corrective should look natural yet vibrant. Lips do not need to look plain, eyes can look colorful, and cheeks can look bright. The focus of this makeup is to even out the skin tone, round out the features, and soften the face. No matter the gender, the following steps will help visually change the face, drawing details away from naturally occurring masculine features.

Step 1: Concealer

Unlike with masculine corrective, feminine makeup starts with concealer. Evaluate the face and determine if there are any areas that need to be covered using the techniques described in Chapter 7.

- Apply the concealer to any areas that stand out from the natural skin tone. Areas could include blemishes, dark circles under the eyes, age spots, birth marks, etc.

- Use powder to set the makeup and prep the skin for the foundation color.

Step 2: Foundation

- Apply a thin layer of foundation over the skin and down onto the neck. Spotlights can wash out performer's features and make faces appear pale. To counter this effect, it is acceptable to match the skin tone or go a shade darker. Going a shade lighter for this makeup is not advisable. Choosing a foundation color can be easier if the colors of the stage lighting are known beforehand.

- Set the foundation with powder and a powder puff.

Step 3: Contour

- There is one main convention to understand before applying feminine corrective makeup. Where masculine corrective relies on angles, feminine corrective accentuates or creates smooth curves on the face – an essential role in drawing distinction between male and female characters. Contouring is the first and best way in drawing this distinction.

- Apply contour color to the following places: cheekbones, jawbone, chin, forehead, and nose.

  A. **Cheekbones**: Use fingertips to explore the cheekbones before placing this contour. Follow the Zygomatic bone from the middle of the ear around to the apple of the cheek.

    - Use contour color to create a soft line starting at the middle of the ear and curving toward the cheek. The line will fade away the closer it gets

to the nose and should not connect to the nostril. Now blend this line up and soften underneath. The darkest part should be nearest the ear then faded softly toward the nose (see Figure 11.9).

  B. **Jawbone**: Use fingertips to find the jaw points below the ears. It should be prominent especially if the jaw is clenched. If the jawline is naturally rounded, apply contour color under the jaw and blend it down onto the neck while softening it onto the face. If the

FIGURE 11.9 *Blended cheekbone contour.*

Credit: Zeek Creative

jawline is square, place contour color under the jaw but also put some slightly on top of the point. Remember that everywhere contour color is applied will appear to recede in space. This gives the illusion that the jawbone is rounder than it is naturally.

C. **Chin**: Add emphasize to the chin by adding a small downward curve of contour color between the lower lip and the ball of the chin. This merely helps to create definition, so lightly fade this line out. It should not be bold or dark. A strong chin is not the goal for feminine corrective; a subtle suggestion of definition is.

D. **Forehead**: Working on our convention for rounded shapes, contour color can refocus the shape of the forehead making it appear thinner and rounded at the top. If the forehead is naturally square or broad, or if the hairline recedes, the forehead contour can help bring focus away from the hairline and down into the face. If the forehead is smaller however, then this contouring step is not necessary.

- Start by applying contour to the sides of the face above the temples and draw the color up around the corner of the hairline. Applying color to the top center of the hairline is not needed as the goal is to make the forehead appear slender. Now blend the contour color out and back toward the hairline and soften

it toward the face. The darkest part of the contour should be at the diagonal points of the forehead, then blended up and down from there (see Figure 11.10). If done successfully, the face will appear rounded or oval.

E. **Nose**: Use contour to reshape the nose if necessary. If the nose is wide, applying color to the sides makes it appear narrower. If the nose is thin, adding contour further on the sides will make it appear fuller. After deciding on the

FIGURE 11.10 *Blended forehead contour.*

Credit: Zeek Creative

shape and whether to define it or not, apply a small amount of contour color to both sides of the dorsum and blend out toward the face. Now soften along the bridge leaving the dorsum free of contour. This should not be a bold color as the nose is already the most three-dimensional object on the face.

Use translucent facial powder, along with a powder puff, to set the makeup now that all the contour color has been applied.

Step 4: Highlight

- Follow the continual rule: Wherever contour is applied, highlight color should be applied as well. Choose a highlight color that complements the foundation but is lighter by several tones. Keep in mind that no matter how pale the complexion, plain white should never need to be used. Consider mixing in the foundation, adding white if needed. For darker skin tones make sure to have a golden tone in the highlight. Going too light in the highlight can make dark skin look dry. Test the colors on the neck or jaw before settling on a highlight color. It is helpful to write the mixture of foundation color down on a makeup chart for later reference.

- Apply highlight color to the following areas: cheekbones, jawbone, chin, forehead, and nose (see Figure 11.11).

  A. **Cheekbones**: Apply highlight to the apple of the cheeks, blending it out in all

FIGURE 11.11 *Highlight marking.*

Credit: Zeek Creative

directions. This should be a soft, subtle effect. Blend it into the contour color so that both merge together.

  B. **Jawbone**: Plant highlight along the edge of the natural or new jawline above the contour line and soften. The color will be on the face either way and not under the jawbone. Stage lights will reflect off the highlight and help change the shape of the face.

  C. **Chin**: Apply a light application of highlight to the ball of the chin and blend outward.

If the chin is not naturally strong and the desire is to make it appear larger, blend the highlight down further and slightly under the chin. The lighter color increases the perception that the chin is larger in length.

D. **Forehead**: Use highlighting to make a small forehead appear larger in the opposite way that contouring helps reduce the size of larger foreheads. Apply highlight color to the center of the forehead and blend it out toward the sides. It is acceptable to apply color to the outside edges near the hairline and soften. This highlight is always soft and subtle. If the forehead is naturally large this step is not necessary.

E. **Nose**: Highlight is imperative if you applied contour to reshape. For a thinner nose illusion, apply a small strip of highlight color down the dorsum and fade it into the contour on both sides. For a wider nose illusion, apply highlight not only on the dorsum but a little on the sides. Then blend it into the contour to give the appearance of width. Whether changing the shape of the nose or emphasizing the natural shape, adding a strip of highlight down the center is a good idea.

Powder all the areas where highlight was applied.

Step 5: Eyes

Most any audience member will note that seeing a performer's eyes is essential to their experience. It is imperative, as a performer or makeup artist, to do whatever is needed to make the performer's eyes appear wide and expressive. Part of any corrective makeup is evaluating if the eyes are too close together or too far apart, whether the eyes are large or tiny, or if the eyes are hooded. Any of these effects can be manipulated with corrective techniques using light, shadow, and a hint of color.

Eyes for stage have their own set of rules. Be sure to consider what the audience needs from the makeup and not necessarily what the model perceives as correct. Remember, stage makeup is different from beauty makeup. Colors, intensities, and facial contours can all change given the character design or the theatrical space.

A. **Highlight**: Start by covering the entire eyelid with highlight color. It should be a soft shade and not too intense. Blend the edges of the color into the lid crease and soften. If the lid crease is not obvious then fade the color up into the foundation where a crease would be. Do not take the highlight up to the eyebrow. If using cream makeup, powder the eyelid to set.

B. **Eyeliner**: Applying eyeliner can be challenging but, with a steady hand, eyeliner will make your eyes pop.

- There are several mediums which can be used for eyeliner such as pencil, gel, cake, or liquid. Any of these will work for feminine corrective. What is important is the shape, not the product being used. Refer to the product guide in Chapter 8 for more details.

- Choose a color that complements the skin and hair color. Pale complexions and lighter hair colors do not need black liner for feminine corrective. Brown or dark brown works better. Dark and mid-range complexions with dark hair or fair complexions with dark hair can use black liner so the eyes will stand out more.

- Start with the bottom eyelash. Place the brush at the inside corner and pull the liner brush or pencil just under the lower eyelashes getting as close to the lashes as possible. Continue to draw the line along the lashes until reaching the outer edge but do not bring it to the very edge of the eye. Stop this line about a quarter inch from the upper lash line. Remember the goal is to make the eye appear as open and wide as possible. By stopping the line before the edge of the eye, the eyelash lines will not be connected. This is a counter-cultural practice; however, for stage it is highly effective.

- Continue with the top line. Before application, open the eye and find where the lashes on the outside curve up and out. Take the liner medium and lightly mark this line. Do not add a wing just yet; only indicate where the angle will be placed. Now close the eye and, starting at the inner corner but not connecting with the lower lash, draw the line along the upper lashes then lightly swoop it along the indicator mark. The line may be a 35-degree or 45-degree angle. It should never be drawn straight out to the side though, and it should not connect with the bottom line. The outer wing should be only about a quarter inch long from the lash line. Eyeshadow will be used to define this line more. If using a wet medium for eyeliner allow it time to dry before opening the eye (see Figure 11.12).

C. **Eyeshadow**: Eyeshadow for stage serves two purposes. It acts as contour for the eyes and draws attention to the eyes. Following are two

FIGURE 11.12 *Upper and lower eyeliner.*

Credit: Zeek Creative

methods of applying eyeshadow. The first is by using powder, and the second is by using cream contour color.

- When using powder, it is best to operate using a three-tone eyeshadow palette (see Figure 11.13). A light color for the highlight, a mid-range color, and a darker color are all needed when applying eyeshadow. The cream highlight color, that has already been applied to the eyelid, is the first step even though it is not a powder. Whether with a powder or cream, the eyelid highlight should be bright. For the mid-range tone, plant the color at the eyeliner wing and blend in the eye crease while lightly fading it toward the lacrimal area. Soften it onto the lid but not completely covering the highlight color. Next, plant the darker tone at the eyeliner wing and softly work it in the crease, overlapping with the mid-range tone but not completely

covering it. This color is only used to add depth and dimension to the eye. While blending both tones together, blend them up toward the eyebrow but do not take the color all the way to the brow. Blend some of the darker tone into the outer eyeliner line and down along the lashes blending it softly toward the center of the eye.

- When using cream contour, plant the color at the eyeliner wing and fade it along the eye crease, blending it lighter as it gets closer to the lacrimal area (see Figure 11.14). Contour color can be added along the eyeliner line as well. Be sure to blend the color softly into the highlight, not eliminating the light color completely. Blend the color up toward the brow but do not go all the way. Also, do not let the eyeshadow connect to the lacrimal area, but allow the color to fade into the highlight tone.

FIGURE 11.13 *Powder eyeshadow blending.*

Credit: Zeek Creative

FIGURE 11.14 *Cream eyeshadow blending.*

Credit: Zeek Creative

D. **Additional highlight**: There is a small area where additional highlight can be applied to make the eyes appear wider. Take a small amount of highlight color and apply it at the outer eye between the upper and lower eyeliner lines. There should be an eighth-inch gap already there, a perfect spot to apply the light color. This spot of highlight can be a bold tone but ensure it is softened and not stark. Plant the color, then blend it underneath the eyeliner wing.

E. **False eyelashes**: False eyelashes are fun but not always a necessity. Using them can add an extra pop to the eyes and encourage the illusion of big and bold features. Before reaching for the longest pair, a couple of elements must be evaluated. The first is show design. Time periods may dictate thickness or style of the lashes. The second is the size of the house and stage. The closer the audience, the more natural the eyelashes; the larger the audience, the larger the lashes. No matter the choice, applying them is exactly the same.

• Before application, determine if there is a latex allergy to consider. Many eyelash adhesives are latex based, so check the box first.

• There are two ways to apply the adhesive to the lash line. The first is using the applicator directly and dragging a small bead of product along the lashes. For the second method, apply a small drop to a makeup palette or to the back of the hand. Gently drag the flat of the false lashes through the adhesive. Whichever method is chosen, once a small line of adhesive is on the false lash line, it is time to apply.

• It is helpful to have the eye parted slightly or lightly closed when applying false lashes. Starting in the lacrimal area, lightly press the flat of the false lashes above the top of the natural lash line. The false lashes will probably overlap the eyeliner lines, or they may land slightly under the eyeliner lines.

After the inner corner is attached, work gently toward the middle of the eye then to the outer corner. When the false lashes are secured press them firmly and allow them to dry. Drying time should only last a minute. Flutter the eyes to make sure the corners are not stuck together with adhesive.

- Once the adhesive is dry and firmly secured, run mascara through the natural lashes and the false ones to blend them together. You may even want to use an eyelash curler to merge the natural lashes with the false lashes. Either way will help create seamless, flashy eyelash lines.

F. **Eyebrows:** The essence of corrective makeup is making the facial features as uniform and symmetrical as possible while emphasizing expression. Getting the perfect brow shape, that is consistent for both, can be tricky. That is why the three keys to stage brows are color, shape, and consistency.

- Before applying the first brush stroke, evaluate what color works best for the complexion. The natural hair color is usually the best; however, eyebrow hair can often grow spotty or sparse. A good rule for stage is this: Brows should be at least two shades darker than the natural hair. This will ensure the eyebrows will be easily spotted from the audience, and that is a must.

- Next, evaluate their shape. High arches and curved shapes make the eye appear wider. Flat or straight eyebrows can make the face appear masculine, while angled eyebrows can make a character look angry. Be sure whatever shape is chosen conveys the nature of the character and that the brows are symmetrical.

- If using a matte eyeshadow powder, consider using an eyebrow bristle brush for the application. The stiff bristles help deliver color intentionally without spraying product on other areas of the skin. Start at the inside corner of the brows, follow the hair up toward the arch, and then down toward the outside end of the brow. If using an eyebrow pencil, start at the inside corner and lightly draw the color along the brow accentuating a high arch if desired. Drawing a short series of quick, small strokes may help more than drawing one continuous line end to end. If the brow has a natural angle at the peak, consider using the color to round it out. After an initial pass to determine the shape, repeat this process until the desired color intensity has been achieved. Try to recreate the same effect for both brows so they become consistent *twins*.

- Lastly, go back to the space left between the eyeshadow color in the crease and the eyebrow. Use a light amount of highlight color in that space under the brow where the highest point of the arch would be. This highlight will appear to push the eyebrow higher. Soften this highlight down into the eyeshadow while blending the edges (see Figure 11.15).

FIGURE 11.15 *Completed eyebrow.*

Credit: Zeek Creative

Step 6: Lips

Emphasizing the lips is another important element in a corrective makeup. Lip color and design can change with each performance. Whatever the design or color, use the makeup to bring the lips to life. The following are steps to achieve bold, expressive lips that everyone can see.

A. **Lipliner**: Often people disregard lipliner and underrate its usefulness. There are two important reasons to use lipliner (see Figure 11.16). The first useful quality of liner is that it keeps the lipstick from bleeding onto the skin. The thick consistency of liner acts as a barrier keeping the vibrant color contained to the lips. Wearing lipliner is essential for a performer who is on stage, under lights, for an hour and a half before intermission. The other useful quality of lipliner is that it can achieve dramatic contouring effects otherwise unattainable with lipstick alone.

- Before choosing the liner and lip colors, evaluate the lip shape. For this makeup, the lips should be symmetrical and balanced. If the lips are normally thin, this is an opportunity to fill them out; if the lips are naturally full, then makeup can make them look smaller. Whatever shape is chosen, make sure they are balanced when complete.

- When choosing a liner color, try one that is several shades darker than the lipstick color. The color difference will add dimension when lip color is applied.

- Take the pencil and trace around the lips or draw the new desired shape. Ensure the color is all the way around, paying attention to the lip peaks under the philtrum as well as the mouth corners.

FIGURE 11.16 *Applied lipliner.*

Credit: Zeek Creative

Parting the mouth may help as the liner is applied in the mouth corners.

B. **Lipstick**: With the liner in place, it is time to apply the lip color. When choosing the correct color, refer back to Chapter 9 for determining which color is best to use.

- Scoop the lip color onto a palette, then apply with a brush for best control. As lip color is added to the lips, start blending the lipliner into the outer edges of the mouth. The peaks, corners of the mouth, and lower lip are the best places to create this dynamic two-tone effect. Blending the two colors together will emphasize the natural three-dimensional aspect of the lips. The tonal effect will allow audience members to not only see the lip color, but also see the natural contouring of the lips.

C. **Highlight**: Use a small amount of highlight color and apply small dabs around the corners of the lips. Four areas of the skin around the lips need highlights: on either side of the top lip points and on either side of the bottom lip. The highlight adds emphasis to the lips, controls the shapes, and creates a smooth youthful glow.

D. **Extra**: If the top or bottom lip is naturally fuller then this step is not necessary.

- Take a small dab of highlight with a finger or brush and apply the highlight color to the lower lip, lightly blotting until it blends with the color. The effect should create a pouty lower-lip effect. If your upper lip is thinner, consider applying a small dab of highlight to the top points and not to the bottom lip. Adding highlight to both top and bottom lip is not necessary.

Step 7: Blush

The finishing touch on feminine corrective makeup is blush. Makeup allows for total control over facial color. The purpose of foundation and concealer is to even out the skin tone and correct any redness or color abnormalities. Blush adds the color back into the face, giving health and glow to the features.

- When applying blush, a large natural-haired brush works best. Choose a color that would be a natural flushed tone. It may help to reference Chapter 4 in choosing the best color for the makeup.

- Once the desired color has been chosen, put product on the brush and give it a shake removing excess color. Now, gently brush the blush from the cheekbones at the ears down to the apples of the cheeks. Plant the color on the Zygomatic highlight but let it merge into the contour color. Control the color ensuring that the tones are not too vibrant, but subtle and rosy. Use the same motions at the jawline. Apply the blush to the same area where contour color was applied under the jawline, rounding out the jawbone. Pull the color behind the ear and onto the neck, while fading it under the chin.

- Move to the forehead. If the forehead was shaped with contour around the edges, apply blush in the same spots. Gently brush the color around the hairline edge, stopping it above the temples.

FIGURE 11.17 *Completed application.*

Credit: Zeek Creative

- Lastly, use a small amount of product and give the nose and chin a quick, single swipe. Do not apply too much to these areas, or the blush color will negatively affect the makeup. By following these steps, the face should have a healthy glow, and the feminine corrective makeup will be complete (see Figure 11.17).

CHAPTER 12

OLD AGE MAKEUP

The ability to make a young person appear older has been used countless times on stage and in films. In the theatrical world, professional venues will not hire a young person to play an older character but will generally hire for the age of the character. The trick comes when characters age throughout the course of the play or performers need to play different characters. Knowing how to alter facial features with wrinkles and folds is a vital skill for thespians and for makeup artists. Whether doing a complete old age application or picking several techniques to simulate middle-age, performers should be able to execute the steps to make their character convincing.

The following steps will describe how to apply a complete old age application. Any of these elements can be used to age a character. The more intense the makeup, the older the person will appear. Experiment to see which effect works best for the role intended.

Step 1: Foundation

As people age, their skin color changes. When choosing a foundation color, chose one that is either the same as the natural skin tone or a shade or two darker. Remember that the stage lights will brighten the skin, so the darker skin tone will help. Also, this makeup includes many places for highlight and contour and using a darker tone will aid in dynamic blending.

- Apply foundation to the face and onto the neck with a makeup sponge. Older skin can appear blotchy, so consider applying an uneven foundation coverage. If using a darker foundation tone, blend it past the jawline and fade it into the natural skin tone.

- Apply a light layer of makeup over the eyebrows and lips. Both eyebrows and lips lose intensity over time, and this will help de-emphasize these areas.

- Powder the foundation color to set the makeup.

Step 2: Contour

When skin ages, fleshy firm areas of the face start to sag, creating wrinkles. Many individuals find that the top part of their face – the forehead and temples – and the natural bony areas become more noticeable and sunken. Old age contour helps define the natural bone structure while creating wrinkles that have not yet developed in more youthful skin. These contour points emulate the bone structure of masculine corrective placements to some extent, while also creating areas of sagging wrinkles. Feel free to refer back to Chapters 10 and 11 for a more in-depth description of these first few contour points. For an old age application, initial contour color will be applied to the following areas: brow bones, temples, cheekbones, nasolabials, philtrum, mouth, jawline, chin, upper eye slopes, lower eye bags, and concern lines.

A. **Brow bones**: Place contour color in a curving "L" shape, following the natural brow bone, while blending the line toward the forehead. Soften the line onto the bone. This should not be a strong contour – merely a suggestion of an indention (see Figure 12.1).

B. **Temples**: Find the temple indention and apply contour in a "C" shape. After planting the color, blend back toward the hairline while softening the harsh edge toward the brow bone and around toward the cheek.

C. **Cheekbones**: Start at the middle of the ear and place contour color in a curved right angle under the cheekbone curving down where the teeth and the Masseter meet. The effect is a hollow, sunken cheek. This shape is similar to the masculine corrective cheek contour except it is more intense for this makeup. In "Bone Structure," it would be as if you left off the left arm of the "y." Be sure not to draw this line all the way to the jawline. The line should stop about two inches above the jaw. After the color is placed, blend the top of the contour

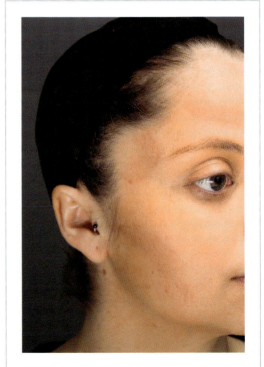

FIGURE 12.1 *Blended brow bone, temple, and cheekbone contours.*

Credit: Zeek Creative

curve up while blending the bottom of the curve back toward the jawbone. Soften the lines on the opposite sides of the blending to eliminate harsh lines.

D. **Nasolabials**: Locate the fleshy areas of skin on either side of the nose that appear when smiling. Often referred to as *smile lines*, the nasolabial folds can be easily contoured to create an old age effect. Start by applying contour at the nostrils. Drag the color along the wrinkle – down and out. Let the color fade away as it moves down toward the mouth. Be careful not to curve the line beside or under the nostril but bring it out and down from the nose. The line does not travel all the way down to the chin. If this happens, the line cuts off the mouth from the rest of the face creating a ventriloquist puppet effect. Once the color is planted, blend the contour line up. Remember that there are no harsh lines on the face. The underside of the

nasolabial contour lines can be intense but soft. Lightly soften the line on the underside toward the philtrum (see Figure 12.2).

E. **Philtrum**: Apply a small amount of shadow to the small divot under the septum. Located on the upper lip, this area already has natural dips and hills. Applying contour here emphasizes the ridges of the philtrum making it seem fleshier and wrinkled.

F. **Mouth**: Notice the very edges of the mouth corners. A small area of shadow color can be added here to create a big effect. At the very corners of the mouth, add contour color in a small downward stroke. The color is very intense, but the line is small – only about a quarter inch. The effect deepens the natural indention of the mouth making it appear as if it is sagging.

G. **Jawline (jowls)**: Place thumb and index finger on either side of the ball of the chin. These are

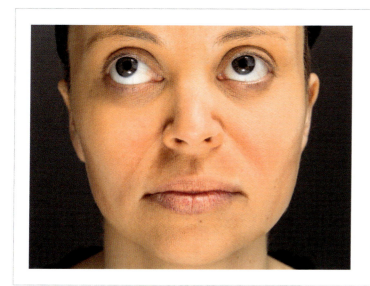

FIGURE 12.2 *Blended nasolabials, philtrum, and mouth contours.*

Credit: Zeek Creative

the two points to emphasize when contouring the jawline to create jowls.

• Start by drawing a small arrow right at the points where the fingers were positioned on either side of the chin. The arrows should point up and fade under the jawline.

• Place the brush at the jaw point under the ear and drag the color in a rounded, sagging shape toward the chin arrows. Connect the line with the arrow point. The jawline should be over-drawn, sloping down past the normal jawbone. This effect takes away the square shape of the jaw and replaces it with a soft, sagging effect.

• Blend the jaw contour down toward the neck and soften up toward the face. The arrows beside the chin should blend and soften, taking on the appearance of

indentions and not realized arrows. Using a sponge to blend is the best technique to smooth the contour color onto the neck as this line can be difficult to see (see Figure 12.3).

H. **Chin**: Follow the natural downturn of the mouth by placing shadow below the lip and above the chin ball. Lightly blend this out in a sideways "C." The shape should mimic the curve of the mouth contour and the nasolabial line – emphasizing sagging skin around the mouth.

I. **Upper eye slopes**: De-emphasize the eyes by creating sagging features with shadow color (see Figure 12.4). One of the goals of old age makeup is to make the eyes look weaker and less intense. There should already be foundation on the eyebrows; adding a sloping eye bag to the top of the eye will weaken the eye and angle the features.

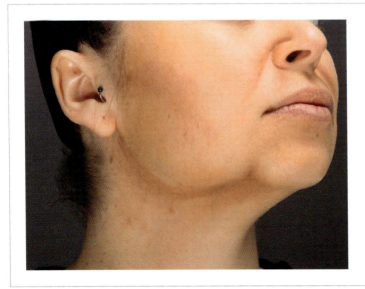

FIGURE 12.3 *Blended jowl contour.*

Credit: Zeek Creative

- Draw a diagonal line directly under the inner corner of the eyebrow to the outer corner of the eye. The line slopes over half of the eyelid and follows the eyelash line for a quarter of the eye. Be sure not to let the diagonal line fall into the eyelash crease.

- Finish the line by overshooting the outer corner and sloping it diagonally from the edge. The diagonal line should extend past the eye corner about one quarter of an inch. This extension is very important as it emphasizes the slope of the eye.

- Shade the area underneath the diagonal line, blending it toward the lacrimal area. This color does not need to be intense, only a light darkening of the area. Once the color is blended toward the nose soften it away. Color should not be intense in the lacrimal area. Soften it and allow the color to fade.

J. **Under-eye bags**: Locate the area of skin underneath the eye. This is where the eye bags are located. Eye bags come in many different shapes and look more natural when they are not uniform. Asymmetrical shapes and varying intensities make eye bags look more natural.

- Determine what shape already exists under the eyes and emphasize it. The shape could be diagonal or curved like a half-moon. Whatever the shape, place the brush at the lacrimal area below the eye and draw the shape curving it down and around to the outer corner of the eye. Do not connect the eye bag shadow with the upper eye slope contour.

- Blend the contour color up while maintaining a softened intense line on the bottom. Consider varying the intensity of color so the color is not consistent the entire length of the eye bag (see Figure 12.4).

- Locate the small indention where the eyeball sits in the socket. Place a smaller line of shadow underneath this pocket and blend up. This contour sits inside the larger eye bag contour and breaks up the smooth surface just below the eye.

K. **Concern lines**: The glabella is the area between the eyebrows where the concern lines are located. When the brow is furrowed, several wrinkles appear no matter the age of the person. As individuals age, these lines become a permanent addition to the face. Creating them when there are no natural wrinkles to follow can be tricky, and there is no formula for application.

- Use a small brush to draw one line, curved slightly, toward one lacrimal area and let the second line curve the opposite way. Both lines float between the eyebrows and are not connected to any one area. The lines are about one-half inch long.

- Blend the contour color upward. When they are finished, the lines should be soft with a more intense line of contour color below.

Once the initial contours have been placed, use a powder puff to press powder into all contour applications.

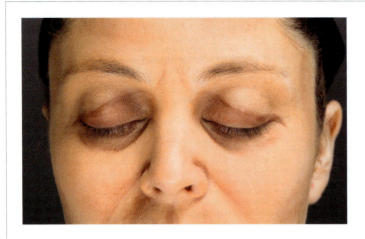

FIGURE 12.4 *Upper eye slopes, lower eye bags, and concern line contours.*

Credit: Zeek Creative

Step 3: Highlight

Wherever there are shadows, there should be highlights. Nowhere is this truer than in an old age application. The intensity of the highlight can vary depending on the prominence of the wrinkle. Keep in mind that deep shadows usually have strong highlights. Highlight color will go in the following areas: brow bones, cheekbones, nasolabials, philtrum, jawline, chin, upper eye slopes, lower eye bags, and concern lines (see Figures 12.5 and 12.6).

A. **Brow bones**: Place the highlight on the brow bone between the brow contour and the temple contour. The color should go on the apex of the bone and soften into the contour colors on both sides.

B. **Cheekbones**: Apply highlight along the apples of the cheeks and soften. This is not an intense color but a general wash of highlight to emphasize the contoured cheek.

C. **Nasolabials**: Apply highlight under the nasolabial contour lines. Plant the color under the shadow and blend onto the upper lip. Similar to the shadow color, this highlight can be a pocket of intense color, but remember to soften it into the shadow.

D. **Philtrum**: Place highlight color on the fleshy peaks of the philtrum. This effect emphasizes the high points of the upper lip.

E. **Jawline (jowls)**: Find the new contoured jowl line. Place the highlight color along the rounded shadow line – under and on top of the natural jawline – then soften it together while blending it into the new jowl. This highlight accentuates the contour of the new jowl while flattening the natural curve of the jaw.

F. **Chin**: Apply a small amount to the chin and soften. Bringing the highlight down toward the jowl emphasizes the shadow color.

G. **Mouth**: Place a light application of highlight under the contoured mouth crease and blend into the chin contour. This effect makes the mouth seem to sag around the edges.

H. **Upper eye slopes**: Apply a generous amount of color to the corner of the eye on top of the sagging eye slope. This highlight should begin in the middle of the eye and go down past the outer corner. By lightening this area, the highlight eliminates the natural indention of the eye and flattens out the sagging eye area.

I. **Under-eye bags**: Place highlight under the eye bag contour. Inconsistency is key here, so vary the amount applied alternating soft blending in spots and intense pockets in others. Blend the highlight down. Next, apply a small amount of highlight under the inner eye pouch just below the lower eyelash contour. This will be a soft highlight.

J. **Concern lines**: Plant highlight color under the contour concern lines located at the glabella. Much like the nasolabial folds, these lines can be intense and softened down.

After completing these steps, powder the highlight colors using the powder puff.

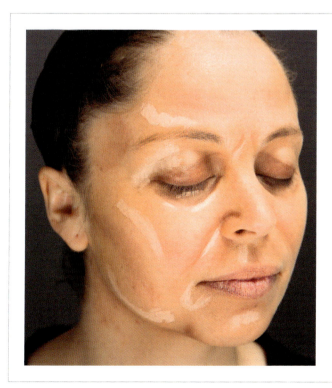

FIGURE 12.5 *Highlight marking.*

Credit: Zeek Creative

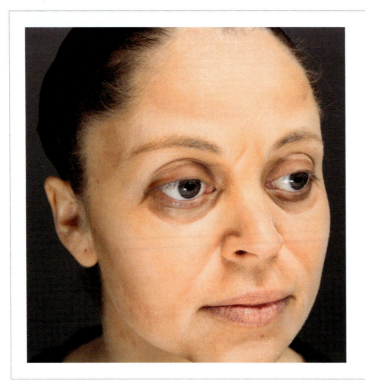

FIGURE 12.6 *Highlights blended.*

Credit: Zeek Creative

Step 4: Crow's feet

Details can turn the most mundane makeup into a creative masterpiece. The first detail to add are the crow's feet. When adding these lines, try not to put them at the corner of the eye. Instead, add two lines to each eye bag breaking the line of the bag. Applying more than two lines can make the eye look cluttered and muddy. Using a flat brush, take the shadow color and quickly swipe it diagonally through the outer edge of the eye bag bisecting the outer line. The direction of the crow's feet should mimic the line of the upper eye slope. These small wrinkles can be bold thin lines as they are usually sharp creases on older faces.

Next, take the highlight color and add bold, yet soft strokes under each contour line. The length of both lines should be approximately one inch long (see Figure 12.7).

Step 5: Forehead wrinkles

Forehead wrinkles can be very tricky. Without practice, they easily look like lines on the forehead. Poor application will destroy the natural effect already created by the makeup. With practice, however, they can be an essential part in making the old age makeup come alive. The key is patience and practice.

FIGURE 12.7 *Crow's feet.*

Credit: Zeek Creative

- Using a thin, flat brush, apply contour color in broken lines from one brow bone to the other. It is more convincing to have them flow over the bone in some spots than keep them contained within the forehead area. Laying the bristles flat to the skin helps create a series of uneven lines across the forehead. Three wrinkles are usually enough. Make sure that the hard line is at the bottom and each contoured wrinkle is blended up. There should be pockets of intensity and pockets of light shading.

- Apply uneven amounts of highlight color under each wrinkle line. This too should be heavier in spots and lighter in others. The blending should be soft underneath each contour line. Remember, keeping the wrinkles asymmetrical is key (see Figure 12.8).

- Set the makeup with powder.

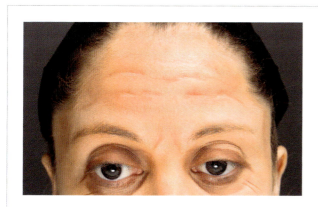

FIGURE 12.8 *Forehead wrinkles.*

Credit: Zeek Creative

Step 6: Extras

Adding small details will make this old age makeup more convincing. These extra techniques will bring the makeup from mundane to realistic. Be careful however. When doing your application, consider only using two or three extra techniques. Overuse will cause the makeup to look busy and overwhelming.

A. **Broken capillaries**: This is a very subtle technique to simulate small areas of broken capillaries around the nose and cheeks. Lightly dab a stipple sponge into maroon cream makeup. Plant the sponge on the capillary area and gently swipe the sponge in one direction. Replant the sponge and swipe in the opposite direction. Repeat action several times on the dorsum and the cheekbones under the eyes (see Figure 12.9).

B. **Veins**: Much like what 18th century women did to simulate translucent skin, adding veins will also give the appearance of translucent skin in an old age application. Start by choosing a navy-blue cream or a steel-gray cream. Using a thin flat brush, apply a lightning pattern design at the hairline either over the brow bone ridge or on the high cheekbone underneath the temple. The vein should be faint and only about two inches long. Veining is a subtle technique but very effective for close-up viewing.

C. **Liver spots (age spots):** These small areas of discoloration can appear in several places

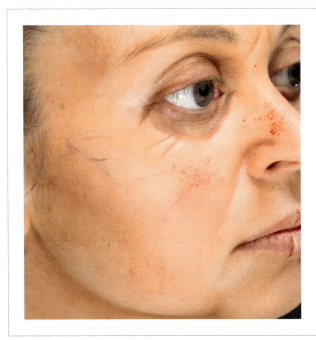

FIGURE 12.9 *Broken capillaries and veining.*

Credit: Zeek Creative

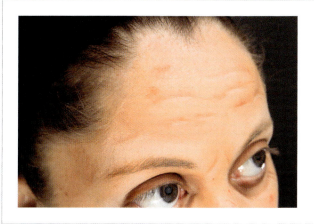

FIGURE 12.10 *Liver spots (age spots).*
Credit: Zeek Creative

around the face. For stage, it is best to keep them confined to the outer areas of the face. Otherwise, they will look like a disease or large moles. Appropriate places to apply them are on the forehead along the hair line, around the temples, or on the bone at the outside corner of the eye (see Figure 12.10). No matter where they are applied, only keep them in that area. Overuse will destroy the effect.

- Start by loading a brush or index finger with a small amount of contour color. Dab the applier softly on one spot of the face. Be sure not to make the spot too big or round. Age spots are often oval or misshapen masses.

- Place a second spot near the first but vary the size and shape. Keep both of the spots subtle. They are not bold applications but light suggestions of color.

D. **Moles**: Moles are simple effects, but inconsistency is key. Only plan to make one or two moles; any more will destroy the makeup. Use the point of a brown eyeliner pencil and place a dot in the desired location. Next use a small brush and add a small amount of black or gray cream makeup to the underside of the colored dot. This color represents shadow and suggests dimensionality.

E. **Cracked lips**: Without consistent care, lips will become pale, cracked, and flaky. There should be foundation already over the lips, but use the initial foundation sponge to add more to the lips and powder. Next use shadow color and add two to four lines in the cracks of the upper and lower lips. These lines should start on the lips but travel past the lip perimeter. Soften the lines so they are not too stark. Now take highlight color and dab a small amount next to each contour mark. The effect should make the lips look parched and cracked (see Figure 12.11).

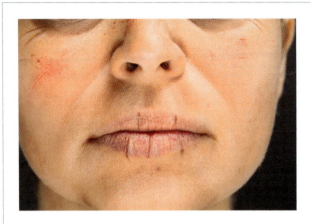

FIGURE 12.11 *Cracked lips.*

Credit: Zeek Creative

Step 7: Texture

One aspect that sets older faces and younger faces apart is texture. Younger skin has not experienced the sun, wind, and years similar to older skin. The easiest way to create this detailed effect is with the stipple sponge. Because of its porous nature, the stipple sponge adds hundreds of small pockets of color to the skin.

- Take the stipple sponge, plant it in the shadow color, then dab the excess off on the palette or on the back of a hand. There should be several layers of subtle applications, so start off light and build up the color.

- Dab quickly at the skin with the sponge in the contour areas first – cheekbones, brow bones, temples, and jowls. After doing a few subtle applications, slowly apply contour stipple to the highlight and foundation areas of the face. They will not be as bold as in the contoured areas.

- Use the same area of the sponge and load it with highlight color, dabbing off the excess

as before. It seems counterintuitive, but remember, anywhere there is recessed

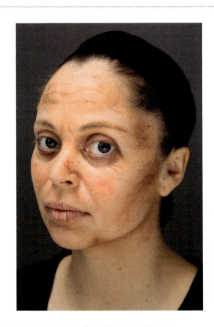

FIGURE 12.12 *Completed application.*

Credit: Zeek Creative

texture there are highlights. That is the essence of the texture technique – thousands of small bumps on the skin that years of exposure have created. Blend the highlight areas and the contour areas of the face together using this technique. The sponge can even be dabbed into the foundation makeup to add this color to the texture. Continue this process until achieving the desired texture range.

- **Warning**: It is easy to create accidental dark spots. If excess makeup is not dabbed off before application, a dark pocket of color could be applied to the face destroying the makeup. Also, overusing the stipple sponge will make the makeup look muddy and hide the detail work underneath. Keep it subtle but make the application intentional.

CHAPTER 13

CONCEALING EYEBROWS

For stage performances or specialty makeups, concealing the eyebrows may be necessary when changing eyebrow shapes. In this book, the next several applications will require some level of concealing the brows. Before diving into those makeups, try practicing the concealing techniques first. Once proficient, consider adding the other makeup elements.

Concealing the eyebrows is similar to concealing tattoos. Both take patience and persistence, but the technique is effective. Several products are required before starting. The first item is a water-soluble glue stick. Whether purple or clear, make sure the glue will wash out with soap and water. Translucent face powder and a powder puff are also needed. Lastly, an undertone color – burnt orange, burnt red, or pink – is needed along with whatever foundation color is desired.

Step 1: Applying glue

The most important thing to remember about gluing down eyebrow hair is that every section of the hair must be covered with adhesive. Product should be layered onto the hair, down to the root, on all sides. This can be tricky, so follow the gluing steps listed here carefully.

- Start by brushing the eyebrow hair backward with the glue stick. Backcombing the hair plants adhesive on the underside of the hair covering the roots.
- Use the stick to brush the hair down toward the eye, and then brush it up toward the forehead. This allows the product to cover the sides of the hair (see Figure 13.1).
- Firmly use the glue stick to splay the hair up and out toward the forehead. Do not lay the

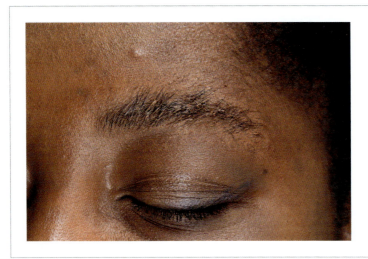

FIGURE 13.1 *Eyebrow hair glued flat.*

Credit: Zeek Creative

eyebrow hair along the natural eyebrow line. Doing this will create a small ridge where the hair is stacked on itself. The goal is to make it as flat as possible, so the natural texture will not be noticed.

Step 2: Applying powder

A translucent powder is important to set each stage of the concealing process. Once the glue has dried, load a powder puff with the powder. Use a generous amount. Firmly press the powder into the eyebrow and repeat this process until all loose powder is removed. The goal is to completely dry out the glue and create a solid surface. Be sure not to use a powder brush as this will not plant a heavy enough layer of powder and will not press the hairs flatter to the skin.

Step 3: Applying undertone

Skin naturally has a warm undertone. When applying prosthetics or concealing eyebrows or tattoos, it is essential to add warmth to the skin. Selecting an orange-red color will neutralize most eyebrow hair colors. Layer a thick amount of this tone over the hair. Keep the color contained to the hair itself and make sure that the hair cannot be seen through the undertone color. Try not to apply too much to the skin. Keep it contained to the hair itself (see Figure 13.2).

FIGURE 13.2 *Orange undertone applied to eyebrow.*

Credit: Zeek Creative

Step 4: Applying second powder

Just as before, load a powder puff with powder and firmly apply it to the eyebrow.

It is important to cover the undertone color completely before moving on to the next step (see Figure 13.3).

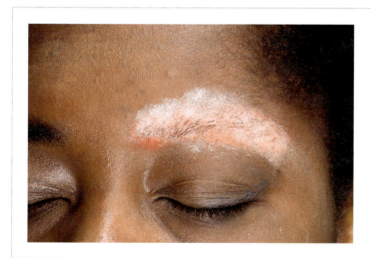

FIGURE 13.3 *Powdered undertone.*

Credit: Zeek Creative

Step 5: Applying foundation

With the undertone and powder in place, adding foundation comes next. A quarter sized amount of cream foundation is required for this step, so make sure enough is mixed before application. Using a makeup sponge, scoop a large layer of foundation color onto the sponge, then lightly apply it to the eyebrow in small dabs. Use the sponge as a small spackle by firmly, but intentionally, planting the product on the brow area. Be attentive not to swipe the makeup across the hair but apply it in firm dabs. Swiping will agitate the brow causing the hair to pull away from the skin. Continue this process until the entire brow area is covered (see Figure 13.4).

Step 6: Applying final powder

Now that the foundation is firmly applied, another strong layer of powder can be applied. Repeat the powdering process as in the previous steps, being careful not to disrupt the makeup.

Step 7: Evaluating

This final step is about evaluating the concealed eyebrow. If small sections of eyebrow hair can still be seen, repeat Steps 5 and 6. The eyebrow should be invisible and completely concealed if done correctly.

FIGURE 13.4 *Completed eyebrow.*

Credit: Zeek Creative

CHAPTER 14

ANGRY MAKEUP

During live performance pieces, the performer must convey emotions with expressions. There normally will not be a time when a director requires an actor to wear *angry* makeup; however, elements from this makeup can enhance expressions or transform the face. Angry makeup is the first of two emotion applications discussed in this book, and one that comes in handy in many circumstances.

This makeup application uses intense focus on the nose, eyes, and eyebrows to emphasize rage or frustration. Using snarling effects and angular brows draws the focus from softer features to angular peaks and lines. Paying close attention to the following techniques will help articulate emotions and create an interesting character.

To build off skills already learned in previous chapters, this angry makeup will use a base makeup of corrective techniques in conjunction with angry elements. This chapter will not review corrective makeup steps. Refer back to Chapter 11 for a refresher if needed.

Step 1: Concealed eyebrows

For this makeup, changing the shape of the eyebrows will help increase the focus of the expression to the eyes. The entire eyebrow will not be concealed though; only the outer half of the eyebrow will be covered. This allows the use of part of the natural brow helping the brow to look more natural and leaving hair exposed.

- Apply glue to the outer half of the eyebrow – the outside tip to the center. Follow the process laid out in Chapter 13 for concealing eyebrows to completely render the outer half invisible (see Figure 14.1).

FIGURE 14.1 *Outer portion of eyebrows concealed.*

Credit: Zeek Creative

Step 2: Foundation

While the glue is drying, and the eyebrow is in process, apply foundation color to the rest of the face. Don't forget to apply foundation down onto the neck and blend it away. Once foundation has been laid over the face and eyebrow, the entire face and makeup can be set with powder.

Step 3: Corrective application

With the eyebrow finished, work on applying the shadow and highlights for a corrective makeup application. Whether using masculine or feminine corrective, apply contours to cheeks, chin, jawline, and forehead areas. Highlights should be in the normal spots as well. If doing feminine corrective, apply eyeliner and eyeshadow as well as lip color. Be sure not to apply blush. That will be saved until the end of the angry makeup application. For a refresher on corrective makeup, look back at Chapter 11 and follow the appropriate steps.

Step 4: Mouth creases

Much like in the old age application, indenting the corners of the mouth changes the angle of the mouth creating different illusions. Angry makeup relies on sharp angles and diagonal lines to create stern features. Remember that when applying each of these effects.

- Apply a small amount of shadow to the corners of the mouth by drawing down in a sharp diagonal line. The crease should be no more than a quarter inch long and should give the mouth a perpetual frown effect. Remember these are not wrinkles but suggestions of a grimace.

Step 5: Nasolabials

The nasolabial region is the best place to utilize angry elements. Applying intense makeup here helps create flaring nostrils and a scornful sneer. Keep in mind that the lines and wrinkles should be vertical and sharp.

A. Plant contour color right above the nostril almost toward the tip of the nose. Curve the color around the nostril, then brush the line down about an inch into the nasolabial fold. This line is not a soft curve like in old age makeup but a sharper diagonal line. It is also not meant to be an actual wrinkle, so be sure not to take it too far down. The contour line should only be about an inch past the nostril.

B. Blend the shadow color up. Starting at the nostril lines, focus the blending upward. Pull the color up toward the eyes while making the color soft. Keep the blending vertical all the way down to the end of the contoured line. The deepest shadow color should be around the nostrils and in the crease beside the nose (see Figure 14.2).

- Be sure the shadow color does not blend right beside the nose. This will make the cheeks look round and not vertical.

C. Apply highlight color to the underside of the contour. Blend this color downward but soften the line, joining the light color with the contour.

Step 6: Lacrimal areas

Part of looking angry is having a brooding appearance. Nothing helps to achieve this more than having a furrowed brow. Bringing this intensity to the eyes draws focus to the brows and will help emphasize the eyebrow shape to come.

- Apply shadow color to the lacrimal area of the eyes, concentrating it to the inner corners before blending it away. Once the color is planted, brush it softly away under the brow bone and down slightly onto the nose. The nose contour does not connect

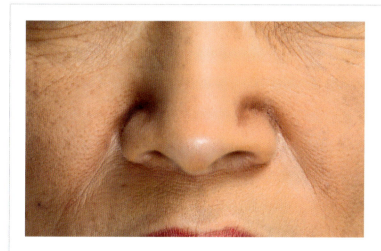

FIGURE 14.2 *Highlight and contour of nasolabial folds.*

Credit: Zeek Creative

with the nostrils. The shadow just softens and fades away. This effect is similar to the masculine corrective technique that adds emphasis to the eye area. The difference with the angry makeup application is that this could be very deep in color; while in the masculine makeup application, it is softer and lighter.

Step 7: Concern lines

When the brow is furrowed, deep concern lines appear in the glabella. These lines help enhance the angry features in the eyes and will connect into the eyebrows when completed (see Figure 14.3).

A. Start in the lacrimal area and draw a small swooping curve up from the lacrimal area toward the forehead. Unlike in other sharp angry lines, these curve low before sharply angling upward. Blend the contour color up slightly and soften the underline.

B. Place highlight color directly under the contour color and fade it down. Place a soft application of highlight color above the concern line contour. Do not place it directly above the contour line but place it where the natural pocket of skin would be the strongest. If done correctly, it will appear as if there are two new pockets of skin protruding from the brows.

Step 8: Eyebrows

The eyebrow direction is key for an angry makeup application, so it is important to get the shape right. Due to this being the first time drawing an eyebrow shape, consider practicing the shape on paper or the back of a hand before starting. The desired shape is an angular curve – a softened triangular shape. The goal is to create a high, sharp arch that dips low at the end. This strong downward angle will bring intensity to the furrowed brow. Be sure to keep the brow natural and stay away from large, boxy shapes.

FIGURE 14.3 *Highlight and contour of concern lines and lacrimal areas.*

Credit: Zeek Creative

A. Start by using the eyebrow medium – gel liner, eyeshadow, eyebrow pencil, cream makeup – to trace the line of the new eyebrow. Begin in the natural brow, the portion left unconcealed, and move slowly up to the desired height of the arch before letting the line dip down toward the outer eye area (see Figure 14.4).

B. Next, using the eyebrow medium, lightly draw the shape of the new eyebrow along the traced line. Starting in the natural hair helps to control the line and makes the new eyebrow look natural. Follow the thickness of the natural brow and continue the same thickness throughout.

C. Last, now that the shape is down, make the brow appear even more natural by drawing tiny hairs through the eyebrow shape. Pay attention to the peak as this will emphasize the new angular design. These little hairs will add realism to the false eyebrow making it appear more convincing (see Figure 14.5).

FIGURE 14.4 *Eyebrow outlined with medium.*

Credit: Zeek Creative

FIGURE 14.5 *Completed eyebrow.*

Credit: Zeek Creative

Step 9: Forehead wrinkles

Forehead wrinkles are yet another way to increase the angular direction of an angry makeup application. These wrinkles, however, are not as deep or severe as the ones created in the old age makeup application, nor do the wrinkles span the entire forehead. Be sure to follow the forehead wrinkle directions spelled out in Chapter 12.

- Notice the angular shape of the new eyebrow. Follow that same shape and create a series of two or three wrinkles directly above each eyebrow. These wrinkles should not connect, but float above the eyebrows. Start them about a half inch above the brows, and then create the others above the first. Remember to keep them inconsistent – do not make them too sharp.

FIGURE 14.6 *Gray applied in cheeks, nasolabials, and lacrimal areas.*

Credit: Zeek Creative

Step 10: Extras

Now that the main features of this makeup are complete, details can be added to make the application come to life. Unlike in the old age application, consider combining all of these extra details to create a unique character.

A. **Depth**: In each of the contour points where wrinkles and folds would be the darkest, a more intense color can be used to softly add stronger dimension. Since this makeup plays on intensity and angles, using a gray or ebony tone will deepen these effects. Use a small amount of color and apply the makeup into the following areas: the nasolabials at the top of the nostrils, the lacrimal areas, forehead wrinkles, and cheek contours. These applications are subtle, so be sure to blend them thoroughly (see Figure 14.6).

B. **Flared nose**: The intent has been to create the illusion that the nose is flared. To aid in this perception, apply a small amount of gray or black cream to the outer edge of the nostrils inside the septum area. Now apply a small amount of highlight color to the outside of the nostrils. This will further the nose-flared effect (see Figure 14.7)

C. **Emphasize brow**: Use a small amount of highlight color to further emphasize the arching eyebrow. With a brush, apply the color right under the high arch of the brow and above the eyeshadow color. This little pop of bright color will make the new eyebrow seem even higher.

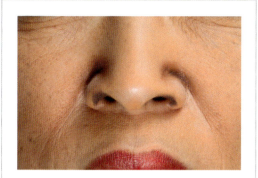

FIGURE 14.7 *Gray used on inside edge of nostrils.*

Credit: Zeek Creative

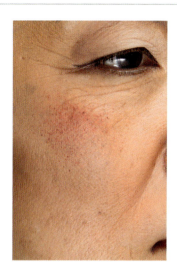

FIGURE 14.8 *Maroon color under eyes and on nostrils.*

Credit: Zeek Creative

D. **Blotchy skin**: When people get angry, inconsistent reddening of the face can occur. This effect can be replicated by using a stipple sponge and maroon or reddish cream colors. Dab the stipple sponge into the color then dab it repeatedly onto the palette or the back of a hand to eliminate excess. With a light application of makeup on the sponge, dab the color onto the cheeks, dorsum, and forehead. Be sure to keep the effect light as this only suggests that color is coming from under the skin (see Figure 14.8).

Step 11: Blush

The final step in this makeup application is to add life back into the face. After determining the correct blush color for the complexion, apply blush into the contour areas first – cheeks, temples, jawline, and forehead. Then, give the nose and chin a quick swipe to finish off the effect (see Figure 14.9).

FIGURE 14.9 *Completed application.*

Credit: Zeek Creative

CHAPTER 15

SAD MAKEUP

The second of the emotion applications is sad makeup. Just like with the last chapter, these techniques may never need to be used at one time. Knowing each technique will aid in transforming a performer, if the production calls for it.

Instead of creating sharp angles as with angry makeup, this application relies on soft and sloped features. Before applying makeup, imagine that there are two invisible dots at each jawline point below the ears. Many of the facial wrinkles and lines will slope toward these imaginary dots. By creating these sloping features, the face can take on a depressing, sad expression. Nothing about this makeup should be angular and harsh.

To build off skills already learned in previous chapters, sad makeup will use a base makeup of old age techniques in conjunction with sad elements. Refer back to Chapter 12 for a refresher if needed.

Step 1: Concealed eyebrows

For this makeup, changing the shape of the eyebrows will help direct the flow of the eyes so they seem to slide off the face. When people are sad or are crying, they tend to scrunch up the glabella region. The eyebrows lift in the center and slide down toward the outside corner of the eye. The entire eyebrow will not be concealed though; only the inner half of the eyebrow will be covered. This allows the use of part of the natural brow helping it to look more natural and leaving hair exposed (see Figure 15.1).

Apply glue to the inner half of the eyebrow – the inside tip to the center. Follow the process laid out in Chapter 13 for concealing eyebrows to completely render the outer half invisible.

Step 2: Foundation

While the glue is drying and the eyebrows are in process, apply foundation color to the rest of the face. Many individuals who are sad, sick, or have been crying can have pale, lighter skin. Consider using a foundation color that matches the

FIGURE 15.1 *Inner portion of eyebrows concealed.*

Credit: Zeek Creative

performer's natural color or a foundation that is a shade or two lighter than the natural skin tone. Do not forget to apply foundation down onto the neck and blend it away. Once foundation has been laid over the face and eyebrows, the entire face and makeup can be set with powder.

Step 3: Old age application

Before working on the sad makeup application, the base makeup can be applied. Using elements of old age to showcase a withered expression is a good place to do this. This step is about applying the contours and highlights in areas that will not be changed by sad elements. Places on the face to apply normal old age techniques are as follows: brow bones, temples, cheekbones, jowls, chin, upper eye slope, and the philtrum.

Step 4: Mouth creases

With the shadow color, lightly indent the corners of the mouth but pull the lines toward the

imaginary points of the jawline. The contoured indentions should only be about a quarter of an inch and appear to pull the mouth out toward the edge. If done correctly, the mouth will appear longer and sloped at the sides. Now take a small amount of highlight and lightly apply it around the mouth crease. This pop of highlight will emphasize the mouth wrinkle and make the mouth look like a frown.

Step 5: Nasolabials

Remembering where the imaginary points at the jaws are located helps focus the lines of the nasolabial folds. These folds will resemble the old age folds more than the angry makeup folds; however, they may not follow the natural smile curve.

- Plant contour color to the top-side of the nostril and pull the line out and down toward the jawline. Be sure not to bring the line too far down as this cuts off the mouth and does

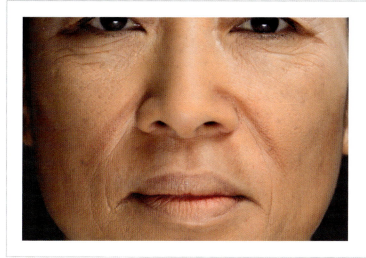

FIGURE 15.2 *Highlight and contour of nasolabial folds.*

Credit: Zeek Creative

not look natural. Once the color is applied, blend up from the line then soften slightly downward (see Figure 15.2).

- Apply highlight color underneath the nasolabial folds, softening it into the contour color.

Step 6: Under-eye bags

The new shape for the under-eye bags can be cumbersome, but the effect is useful to achieve a sad character design. Technique wise, the eye bags are created the same way as in the old age application; it is the shape that is different. With old age makeup, the under-eye bags resembled half-moons or broken angles. When creating the same effect for the sad makeup application, remember the imaginary points at the jawline. It will be as if the half-moon shapes were pushed toward the outer corner of the eyes angled down toward the jaw points. Once these bags are shaped, also apply contour and highlights to

the inner eye bags located under the eye sockets (see Figure 15.3).

Step 7: Eyebrows

The eyebrow shape for the sad makeup application can be difficult to get on the first try. Consider practicing on paper or on the back of the hand before applying makeup to the face. The shape continues the trend of the sloping line. The inner line will start higher than the natural brow, then it will slope down through the natural hairs and trail down toward the imaginary point at the jawline. The eyebrow should look as if the brow is furrowed and the eyebrows are elevated at the inner points before flowing down toward the outside eye (see Figure 15.4).

A. Start by using the eyebrow medium – gel liner, eyeshadow, eyebrow pencil, cream makeup – to trace the line of the new eyebrow. Begin at the inside brow, the

FIGURE 15.3 *Highlight and contour of under-eye bags.*

Credit: Zeek Creative

FIGURE 15.4 *Eyebrow outlined with medium.*

Credit: Zeek Creative

concealed portion, and move slowly down toward the exposed brow hair. Once color has been traced through the natural eyebrow portion, give the end a small tail emphasizing the slope at the ends.

B. Next, using the eyebrow medium, lightly draw the shape of the new eyebrow along the traced line. Starting at the concealed eyebrow, keep in mind that it needs to be the same thickness as the natural exposed hair. Whatever density is chosen, continue that thickness throughout.

C. Last, now that the shape is down, make the brow appear even more natural by drawing tiny hairs through the eyebrow shape. Pay attention to the inner peak as this will emphasize the new sloping design. These little hairs will add realism to the false eyebrow and make it appear more convincing.

Step 8: Concern lines

The concern lines follow the same rules as with the old age application; the only difference being the direction they point. Draw two small lines about a quarter to a half inch long between the new eyebrows. These lines can be almost parallel but should be at different heights, not completely side-by-side. Blend the contour to one side and add a spot of highlight to the other.

Step 9: Crow's feet

Details can emphasize the sloping effect of this emotion makeup. The first detail to add are the crow's feet. When adding these lines, try not to put them at the corner of the eye. Instead, add two lines to each eye bag breaking the line of the bag. Unlike in the old age application, angle them down sharper toward the jawline points.

* Using a flat brush, take the shadow color and quickly swipe it diagonally through the outer edge of the eye bag bisecting the outer line. The direction of the crow's feet should mimic the line of the upper eye slope but angled toward the imaginary jaw dots. These small

wrinkles can be bold thin lines as they are usually sharp creases on older faces. Next, take the highlight color and add bold – yet soft strokes – under each contour line. The length of both lines should be approximately one-inch long.

Step 10: Forehead wrinkles

Done correctly, forehead wrinkles will emphasize the slope of the eyebrows making the expression look weary and depressed. Look back at the instructions in Chapter 12 for a thorough description on creating convincing forehead wrinkles. The only difference will be the shape. Follow the new sloping eyebrow shape, allowing the new wrinkles to slide toward the edges of the forehead before disappearing. Be sure not to connect them all the way across the brow, as this will destroy the realism of the effect. Contour and highlight should be applied; powder to set (see Figure 15.5).

FIGURE 15.5 *Concern line detailing.*

Credit: Zeek Creative

Step 11: Coloration

Adding different tones to the features will help create a detailed character and enhance the story being told. Try using gray and maroon in the following areas to diversify the color palette.

A. **Gray**: Older people or people who are thinner and withered often have a grayish complexion. This comes from a lack of oxygen in the blood and can happen in older adults. Use a light application of gray cream or powder to emphasize the sunken shadows of the face. These shadows could be in the temples, cheeks, jowls, nasolabials, and the outer indentions of the upper eye slope and lower eye bags. Small points of gray could also be intentionally placed in the forehead wrinkles to emphasize depth. Just remember to not overuse the color. The intent is not to wash out the shadow color completely; use it to complement the tones already placed and to draw attention to the deep recesses of the features. Be sure to powder when finished.

B. **Maroon**: Makeup can give the illusion that an individual has been crying or has recently stopped crying. To apply this color, consider using a torn sponge or a finger to dab the makeup.

- Apply a small amount of maroon cream to the nostrils and septum area of the nose. This is a light application to denote that the individual may have been blowing and wiping his or her nose. Try to keep it off of the nose tip, and do not cover the entire nose (see Figure 15.6).

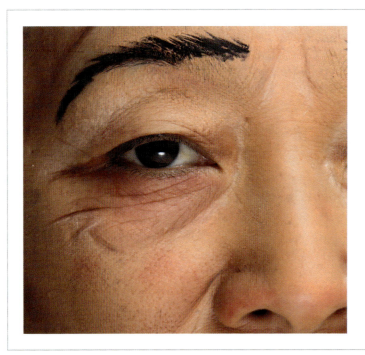

FIGURE 15.6 *Maroon color under eyes and around nostrils.*

Credit: Zeek Creative

- Apply a small amount of maroon cream under the eyes in blotchy patches. The color can go into the under-eye bags as well as around the rims of the eyes. Using a small stipple sponge and following the directions for blotchy skin in the angry makeup application will also achieve the same effect.

Step 12: Extras

Now that the main elements of the sad application are complete, the extra old age details can be applied. These effects can be any of the following: broken capillaries, veins, liver spots, moles, and cracked lips. Apply these effects following the same guidelines as in Chapter 12. Refer back to that chapter for details on application.

Step 13: Texture

Adding texture to the face can transform smooth skin into weather-hardened skin. Be sure to use caution when using the stipple sponge. Once this step is complete, going back and reworking other elements of the makeup is difficult.

- Take the stipple sponge, plant it in the contour color, then dab the excess off on the palette or on the back of a hand. There should be several layers of subtle applications, so start off light and build up the color.
- Dab quickly at the skin with the sponge in the contour areas first – cheekbones, brow bones, temples, and jowls. After doing a few subtle applications, slowly apply shadow color

stipple to the highlight and foundation areas of the face. They will not be as bold as in the contoured areas.

- Use the same area of the sponge and load it with highlight color, dabbing off the excess as before. It seems counterintuitive; however, anywhere there is recessed texture there are highlights. That is the essence of the texture technique – thousands of small bumps on the skin that years of exposure have created. Blend the highlight areas and the contour areas of the face together using this technique. The sponge can even be dabbed into the foundation makeup to add this color to the texture. Continue this process until achieving the desired texture range.

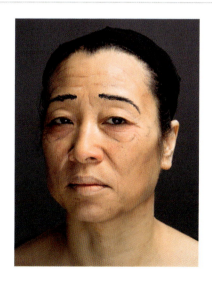

FIGURE 15.7 *Completed application.*

Credit: Zeek Creative

CHAPTER 16

TRAUMA MAKEUP

The term *trauma* encompasses a variety of effects. For theatrical purposes, it means a bruise or wound on the skin. The size and severity of them may vary, but they can be as mild as a small cut or as serious as a severed limb. There is no end to the trauma effects one can create, and it is easy to get carried away with stage blood and fake gore. Before exploring advanced techniques, it is important to master the basics. The standard makeup kit should contain everything needed to achieve these special effect makeups, with the exception of a few additional products. The following is a list of several basic effects and the steps needed to recreate them.

EFFECT #1: BRUISES

Before creating a bruise with makeup, several questions need to be answered.

1. What caused the bruise?
2. Where is the bruise?

3. When did the impact occur?

- First comes the discussion of what caused the bruising effect. If there is a facial bruise, then it is usually caused by an assault by another individual or a solid object coming in contact with the face. Most things that come in contact with the body can leave different bruises. What caused the impact determines the shape of the bruise being created. For instance, punches and kicks will make bruises along with ropes and hard objects. Depending on the situation, impacts with walls and concrete will also leave bruising. The intensity of the impact will also change the intensity of the bruise.

- Second, the location of the bruise must be determined. Different areas of the body will produce a different type of bruise. Color, size, and intensity will all vary depending on the impact's location. For instance, fists make good bruises around the eye areas while hard objects leave bruises and welts on the forehead. Impacts to walls and blacktop can cause bruising on the chin and cheekbones; however, bruising seldom occurs on the fleshy part of the cheeks. When it comes to the neck, the most common theatrical bruise would be a strangulation caused by a hand or rope. The same holds true for arm bruising. These forms of bruising will contain more violets and blues in the early stages, while black eyes will have more pockets of red. Answering this second question produces the majority of information about this trauma effect.

- Last, but equally as important, is knowing when the impact occurred. This can be the trickiest question to answer and may require research to ascertain. Trauma effects are special because they all have a life-cycle. A life-cycle, in this context, means they have a moment of creation where the wound is fresh, then as time goes by, the process of healing occurs. Eventually most trauma effects can heal to a final point, and that would be the end of the life-cycle. For a bruise, this is very important. At impact, and usually a day or two after, bruises are their most vibrant shade. On the face, arms, and neck, bruises are often purple and blue with deep maroon under the skin signifying blood trapped beneath the surface. Over time, as bruises heal, the purple and blue fades giving way to brown and sallow yellows. The last

stages of a bruise are slightly yellow with a tinge of brown before they vanish completely.

- Bruises are very interesting with no two ever alike. While applying bruises to the skin, be sure to make them asymmetrical with pockets of intensity. Following are three major stages of bruising from the moment of impact to being almost healed. The following directions are the same no matter your skin tone. The only difference for darker skin tones would be using a deep golden tone as a substitute for the yellow cream mentioned here. Also remember that no matter the effect, powder when it is finished.

A. Fresh bruises contain the most intense colors. Using a sponge or finger, apply a thin layer of yellow cream to the desired bruise area. When focusing on a black eye, good areas to apply are on the outer corner below the eyebrow and under the eyelid. Also adding color in the lacrimal area will make the bruise look convincing as a place blood naturally pools. Refrain from laying color all the way around the eye. This can look raccoon-like and destroy the effect. Now dab a light to medium layer of violet cream mixed with navy cream. Be creative with this application and make the bruise interesting. After these colors are down, apply pockets of maroon in the lacrimal area or a small amount on the outer eye. Concentrate intensity in spots so the

FIGURE 16.1 *Fresh bruise.*

Credit: Zeek Creative

wound looks uneven and asymmetrical. Try using the stipple sponge; dabbing pockets of violet and maroon onto the wound (see Figure 16.1).

B. Mid-range bruises are in flux between bold fresh colors and the subtle colors of healing. During this period yellow and brown will appear, and maroons will vanish. Start by applying a layer of yellow cream makeup over the area, varying the location just as before. Keep the color restrained to the outer and inner eye areas for best effect. Use brown cream in light spots over the area. Brown tones appear as the maroons and navy colors disappear. They are never dark but subtle shadows of drying blood. Now add light areas of pale violet or navy amongst the brown and yellow makeup. Apply it in different intensities, keeping the original shape. Do not saturate the bruise but keep it light (see Figure 16.2).

C. Healing bruises contain soft colors. A bruise toward the end of the healing process can be light with only fading yellows and browns to denote its existence. When creating an old bruise on stage; however, it still must be bold to be seen by the audience. Start by applying a heavy layer of yellow cream makeup using a sponge or finger. Once applied, use contour color to create dimension and depth to the fading wound. Vary the spots to make them look natural. The brown cream will never be heavily applied, but it should blend well with the yellow to create a realistic fading bruise (see Figure 16.3).

FIGURE 16.2 *Mid-range bruise.*

Credit: Zeek Creative

FIGURE 16.3 *Healing bruise.*

Credit: Zeek Creative

EFFECT #2: CUTS AND ABRASIONS

These effects encompass lacerations, cuts, abrasions, and any other wound where the skin is sliced open using a sharp instrument. The nice thing about abrasions is that they can go anywhere on the body, and the same rules will still apply. The key to making cuts and abrasions believable is inconsistency. If cuts are too straight, they look fake. When determining the best place to apply them, consider surfaces that are curved – the nose, cheeks, eyebrows or lips. Follow these steps to achieve simple yet effective stage effects.

Step 1: Irritation color

- Skin, when irritated, turns pink or red. This is a good first color to lay down. Apply a light coat of pink cream makeup to the area where the cut should be. It is fine to spread it out from the area just a bit, but do not overdo it.

Step 2: Shadow color

- Stage cuts should have a bold outline, so they can be viewed by the audience. Using a sharp, black eyeliner pencil or a thin brush with black or dark brown makeup, trace the shape of the cut. Even if it is supposed to be a straight cut, the edges should be jagged to create a more natural look. When drawing the cut, allow a thin space in the middle. The black not only outlines the abrasion but will double as the shadow tone.

Step 3: Red color

- The center of the black lines is where the tissue is exposed. Apply a blood red color to the inside of the laceration. Keep it concentrated only to the inside of the cut.

Step 4: Blending

- Contour on wounds is still important, and now you can start adding realism. Using a tiny brush, blend small areas of the black line away from the interior of the cut. Don't do it all the way around but vary the blending. Remember, the key to realism is inconsistency.

Step 5: Highlight

- Wherever there is shadow, highlights also exist. Apply a small amount of highlight to small outside edges of the black line. This makes it appear like the skin raises at the edges of the laceration creating dimension (see Figure 16.4).

Step 6: Blood

- If the intent is to create a fresh cut, adding blood will complete the effect. With a small brush, apply spots of blood to the interior of the wound. For a newly created wound, consider what path the blood takes as it drips from the cut. Varying this path creates another layer of realism to the basic trauma effect.

EFFECT #3: SCARS

Scars are simple to create and very effective no matter the skin tone. The most effective scars are old lacerations and cuts that have healed over

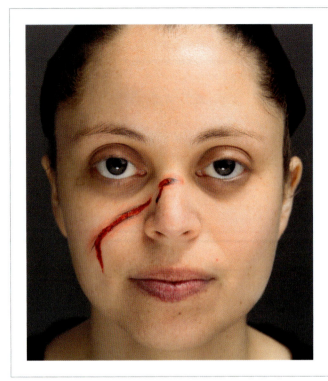

FIGURE 16.4 *Completed cut.*

Credit: Zeek Creative

time. Before getting started, know what created the initial wound and how long it took to heal. Scars can be any shape, just remember the rules for highlight and shadow. The intensity of the colors will vary depending on the size of the performance space.

- For lighter skin tones, use a pink cream tone and place it in a line where you want the scar. Next, apply a broken soft line of highlight color. If you make the line too uniform, it will not look natural. Now use a thin brush to add a light application of contour color under the soft highlight line. This will give the scar

dimension and make the skin appear slightly raised (see Figure 16.5).

- For darker skin tones, apply a soft line of contour color in a broken line. Scars deepen in color on darker skin tones, so the color should be noticeable from the audience. Consider using a thin line of black or ebony inside the contour line in spots to denote depth. Next, take your highlight color and place that underneath the contour color in soft spots. You can even apply highlight on either side of the contour stripe to give the appearance of raised skin on either side of the indention (see Figure 16.6).

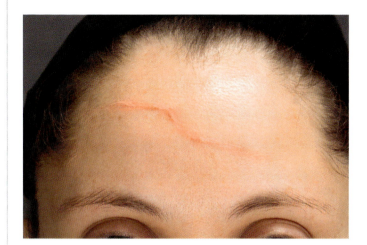

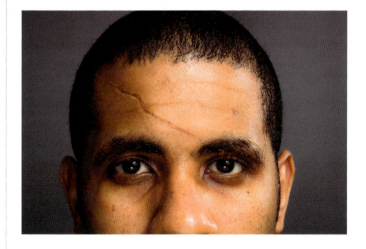

EFFECT #4: BURNS

Some of the best trauma effects contain three-dimensional elements. Burns are a great first-step in exploring this three-dimensional quality. For this application, powdered, unflavored gelatin can be used to create dynamic burns in a short amount of time. Generic brand gelatin can be found at many grocery stores, or pectin – a vegan substitute – may be used as well. Both are sold in small boxes with individual packets inside. For this makeup, a few small packets will be enough. Be sure to have a small cup to mix the product and a stick to stir.

Step 1: Mix the gelatin

- Empty 1 packet of gelatin into a small paper cup. Add one tablespoon water into the gelatin and mix with a small wooden stick or the end of a makeup brush. Water temperature affects how quickly the gelatin solidifies. Using cold water will make the gelatin solidify faster while warm water will make the gelatin solidify slower. The same can be said with the amount of water used. Less water used will make the gelatin lumpier; more water used makes the gelatin smoother. Practice mixing the product before the final application.

Step 2: Apply the gelatin

- Use the stir stick to apply the gelatin to the skin where the effect should be. Do this quickly before it completely solidifies, or the product will not stick to the surface. Make sure the burn area is bumpy and rough. The more texture created the stronger the three-dimensional effect. Consider using multiple applications of gelatin for a severe burn.

Step 3: Add makeup

- Once the gelatin has solidified and cooled, makeup can be applied. When applying makeup to the wound, add it to the skin as well. This will transition the gelatin burn to the skin hiding any seam there may have been (see Figure 16.7).

- Mimic skin irritation from a burn by applying a light coat of pink cream makeup over the area. Using a sponge or brush, apply the color to low and mid-range areas.

- Next, apply contour color or maroon to low areas. This helps to emphasize the depth of the burnt flesh. Once the contour color is applied, add soft dabs of highlight to the peaks of the gelatin. How fresh the burn is determines how the colors will be, so make sure to know the life-cycle of the wound.

Step 4: Detail the wound

- Now that the basic coloring is in place, details can be added depending on the freshness of the wound. Apply a deep red to parts of the lowest areas. These may overlap or blend with the contour color, but that is fine. The wound should appear as if bright flesh is exposed. Once this is complete, dab the stipple sponge into black or dark brown cream makeup. Apply this color sporadically as it will represent the charring of skin.

Step 5: Apply blood

- Adding stage blood is the cherry-on-top. Dip the stipple sponge or makeup brush in a bit of stage blood to give the area a wet smattering of blood. If the burn is fresh, then this is the essential final step (see Figure 16.8).

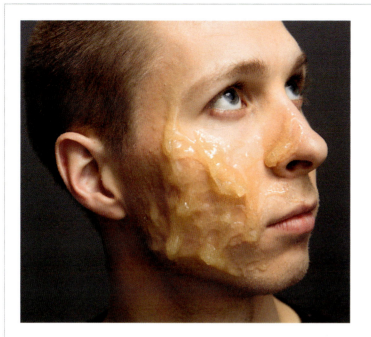

FIGURE 16.7 *Cooled uncolored gelatin.*

Credit: Zeek Creative

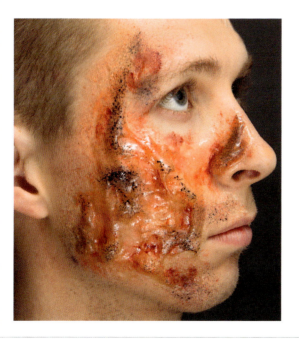

FIGURE 16.8 *Completed burn application.*

Credit: Zeek Creative

EFFECT #5: POPPED PUSTULES AND PEELING SKIN

Creating peeling skin, popped boils, and pustules can transform even the most simplistic makeup into a grotesque creation. These two effects utilize liquid latex and follow similar instruction for application. The following outlines these techniques together and shows how they vary. Please note, if there is a latex allergy then this effect should be avoided.

Step 1: Liquid latex

- Using a brush, apply a moderate layer of latex over the affected area. It will take several layers of latex, but if using thick layers, then only a couple of coats will do. Now use a hairdryer, on the cool setting, and direct it on the wet latex to decrease drying time. This can take three to six minutes, or until the first layer dries completely. After the initial layer has dried, apply a second layer of liquid latex over the first. Repeat the drying process. If there is time to do a third layer of latex, then follow these same steps. The goal is to make the latex thick enough to manipulate. Also, pay attention to the edges since they should be thin and blend into the skin (see Figure 16.9).

Step 2: Add Undertone

- Apply a layer of burnt red or dark pink cream to the dried latex. Allow the color to blend over on the skin to help conceal the transition from latex to skin. Just like with blocking out eyebrows, the red tone adds a natural flush

FIGURE 16.9 *Applying liquid latex.*

Credit: Zeek Creative

under the foundation color. Powder over this, then apply the foundation and powder.

Step 3: Cutting the latex

- At this point determine which effect will be created, then follow the steps listed here (see Figure 16.10).

- A. **Peeling skin**: Using tweezers or fingernails, pick at a small point in the middle of the latex. Now pull the latex away from the skin and use a small pair

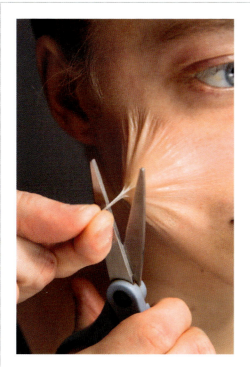

FIGURE 16.10 *Cutting technique for dried latex.*

Credit: Zeek Creative

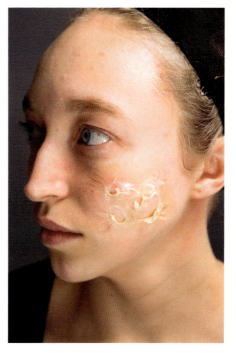

FIGURE 16.11 *Uncolored peeling skin effect.*

Credit: Zeek Creative

of scissors to cut the latex and allow it to bunch or hang. Depending on how serious the wound is, cut and pull whatever bits should be shredded. This will now simulate mangled skin hanging from muscle tissue (see Figure 16.11).

B. **Pustules**: Pustules can be popped boils or other exposed skin diseases. Utilizing the same technique as with peeling skin, pull up a portion of the latex with tweezers or fingernails until there is a section separated from the skin. Now make a clean snip with the scissors, then

let the latex relax. The result should be a rounded hole in the latex exposing the skin underneath. Do the same effect to other areas of the skin and the pock marks will seem inconsistent and a natural progression of an infection. If the makeup calls for multiple pustules, vary the size of each one (see Figure 16.12).

Step 4: Skin coloration

• Now that the under-skin is exposed, it is time to apply the color. Crimson or blood

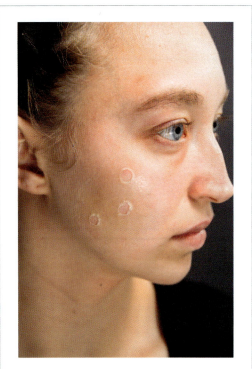

red cream makeups are good colors to paint the under-skin. Using a brush, cover the area inside the holes and underneath the latex. Next use dark brown or black to color the under-edge right at the jagged cut of the latex. This adds a shadow and visually pulls the latex wound away from the bright red flesh underneath. Blend the dark color into the red to add a natural shadow effect. Consider adding a touch of highlight to the outer rim of the latex as another way to visually pull the latex from the skin and increase the three-dimensional quality of the effect (see Figures 16.13 and 16.14).

Step 5: Blood

- To add a freshness to the wound, apply a small amount of stage blood. Using a brush or a stipple sponge, dab blood into the wound. Blood will make the wound look wet and fresh, completing this gory effect.

FIGURE 16.13 *Completed peeling skin effect.*

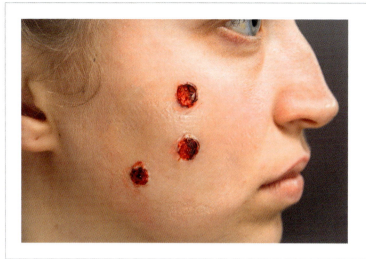

FIGURE 16.14 *Completed popped pustule effect.*

Credit: Zeek Creative

EFFECT #6: EXTRUSIONS

Boils, cysts, large moles, pox, and skin lesions all fall under the category of extrusions. Extrusions are wounds that tend to be isolated and enlarged. Nose putty or wax can be used to achieve these basic, yet convincing effects. These products come in several makeup kit versions, but they can also be purchased at most local costume supply stores or ordered online. A cotton ball and a small amount of spirit gum – a theatrical adhesive also found in most makeup kits – are also necessary to complete this effect.

Step 1: Applying spirit gum

- Determine the location of the protrusion and apply a small amount of spirit gum to the skin. Pull a small amount of cotton from the cotton ball and stick it onto the spirit gum. This small amount will help the putty grip the skin firmly without sliding off (see Figure 16.15).

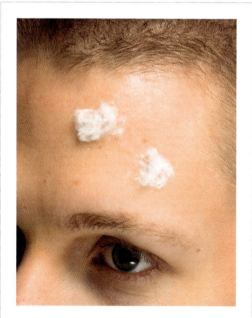

FIGURE 16.15 *Cotton attached with spirit gum.*

Credit: Zeek Creative

Step 2: Preparing putty

*   Roll a small amount of putty or wax between the palms of the hands. This process warms the product and makes it pliable. By the time a small ball of putty has formed, the spirit gum and cotton should be dry and ready to go.

Step 3: Molding the putty

*   Mold the putty onto the cotton while blending the edges onto the skin. Depending on the shape for the wound, there may be a large amount or small amount of putty. While blending, try to make the wax as smooth and seamless as possible. To help smooth the wax, use a very small amount of hair gel. Using gel is a great way to get the putty edges very smooth and thin to the skin; however, using too much gel will cause the putty to run (see Figure 16.16).

Step 4: Using latex

*   Cover the putty in a single, light layer of liquid latex and allow it to dry. The latex gives the makeup a surface to adhere.

Step 5: Applying undertone

*   Apply a layer of burnt red or orange undertone makeup first. This color is essential as it adds natural warmth to the piece. Powder the undertone color on the putty.

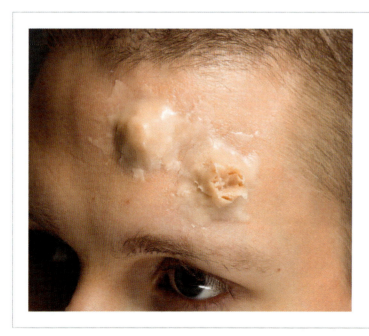

FIGURE 16.16 *Shaped putty for extrusions.*

Credit: Zeek Creative

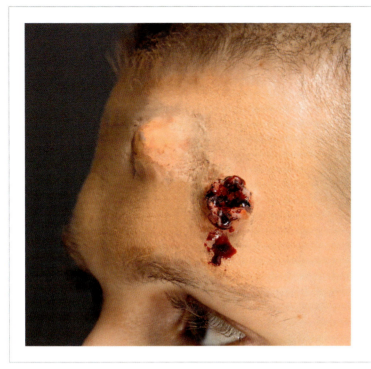

FIGURE 16.17 *Completed extrusions.*

Credit: Zeek Creative

Step 6: Finishing the wound

- Now apply whatever colors necessary to make the wound convincing. Any of the following hues would be great to color the piece: foundation color, yellows, browns, reds, and purples. Be sure to use highlight and shadow where appropriate to make the extrusion stand out (see Figure 16.17).

CHAPTER 17

FANTASY MAKEUP

The basics of stage makeup can be seen throughout the bone structure, corrective, and old age chapters. With angry and sad makeups, emotions and eyebrow manipulation were discussed, and with trauma, different products were utilized to create natural wound effects. Everything discussed up to this point can be used to create fantasy makeup.

When discussing fantasy makeup, the mind usually goes to specialty makeups – ghouls, aliens, sea creatures, monsters, etc. For the purposes of this book, several parameters can be set to focus fantastical efforts, working within the techniques and effects described in this book. Before designing the makeup, try using the two techniques listed as follows.

1. Block out the eyebrows entirely
2. (*a*) Apply a three-dimensional object to the makeup or (*b*) introduce a pattern

EFFECT #1: BLOCKING OUT THE EYEBROWS ENTIRELY

While many fantastical creatures do have eyebrows, it is challenging to eliminate the entire eyebrow completely. Getting rid of the eyebrows is a great first step in creating characters and other science fiction creatures. The previous makeups in this book have discussed the process in detail. Specifically refer back to Chapter 13 for a refresher. Just remember that no matter what color is used to paint the skin, a burnt red or burnt orange needs to be applied to the top of the eyebrow after the glue is dried and powder is applied. The reddish tone adds warmth under the skin and evens out whatever color will be applied on top.

EFFECT #2A: APPLYING A THREE-DIMENSIONAL OBJECT

Nothing characterizes fantastical creatures and effects more than adding outside elements.

Human skin is naturally smooth, but applying textures, ridges, bumps, and scales changes the very nature of the face. Three-dimensional elements can be anything and may be applied in a multitude of ways.

1. **Basic appliqué**: The simplest way to attach a foreign object to the skin is by using spirit gum or liquid latex. Attaching feathers, twigs, and grass work well for woodland creatures like sprites, nymphs, and birds; while rhinestones and gold leaf work well for celestial and fairy creatures.

   • Apply a small amount of adhesive to the skin and hold the object in place until the adhesive dries. Many costume rhinestones will come with adhesive already on the back. These make for easy application but are good for only one use (see Figure 17.1).

2. **Object manipulation**: Creating texture or abnormalities on the skin is a great method for transforming the face. The same techniques mentioned previously can be used or taken a step further. This method works to enhance robots, bumpy monsters, aliens, or anything else with three-dimensional skin.

   • Use products that can be covered with makeup. The shape is what is important not the color. Googly eyes, cooled dots of gelatin, sequins, beads, or cooled hot-glue drippings all fit into this category (see Figure 17.2).

   • Apply spirit gum or liquid latex to attach the element to the skin. Once the glue dries, paint one layer of liquid latex over the pieces so the makeup will grab and not slide off. When the adhesive dries, use a burnt red or burnt orange on top of the element and powder. The applied objects are now ready for whatever skin color desired.

3. **Intrinsic texture**: Applying textured latex to the skin is the best way to create textured skin. This effect is easy to create and lends itself to much creative exploration.

FIGURE 17.1 *Basic application of rhinestones.*

Credit: Zeek Creative

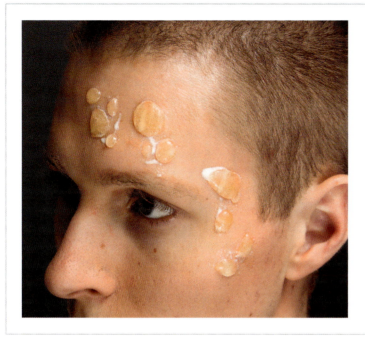

FIGURE 17.2 *Gelatin dots attached with latex.*

Credit: Zeek Creative

- Add small textured substances – beads, tea leaves, coffee grounds – to a small portion of liquid latex. Once it is thoroughly blended, apply the textured liquid to the skin and allow it to dry. After it is dry, apply the necessary makeup to conceal it. Then add color (see Figure 17.3).

4. **Emerging object**: Objects that appear to emerge from under the skin are ideal for creating otherworldly creatures. Horns, bones, eyes, and stones are all examples of objects that could be intrinsic creature parts. You will need to utilize several trauma elements to achieve this effect.

   - Use spirit gum or eyelash adhesive to attach the three-dimensional element to the skin; allow it time to dry completely (see Figure 17.4).

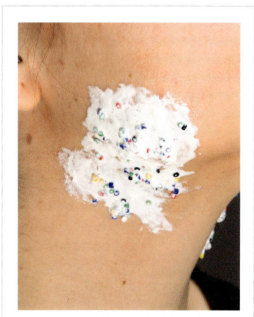

FIGURE 17.3 *Liquid latex mixed with beads for texture.*

Credit: Zeek Creative

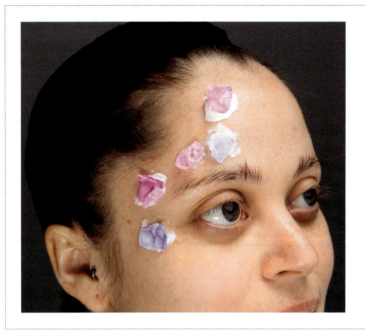

FIGURE 17.4 *Stones applied with liquid latex around the edges.*

Credit: Zeek Creative

- Use either multiple applications of liquid latex around the edges of the piece or use a bead of makeup wax or putty. If using the putty, follow the directions on smoothing and coloring found in Chapter 16. Mold the putty or paint the latex around the piece as if the element is emerging from the skin. Blend the product onto the skin to make it believable.

- Use burnt red or burnt orange on the putty or latex, then powder. The piece is now ready for the chosen skin color.

5. **Hair**: When adding hair as a three-dimensional element, choose a texture that is kinky or wavy. Satyrs, fauns, werewolves, and other amalgamations benefit from hair elements added around the face, chin, and sideburns. Premade prosthetic pieces can also be enhanced with a small amount of hair around the edges. Making the hair look like it is growing from the follicle can be a challenge though, but with patience, it can be convincing.

- Take a small amount of hair and cut it straight across, ensuring hair applied to the skin is all the same length (see Figure 17.5).

- Apply spirit gum or liquid latex to the skin, then lightly touch the hair to the adhesive.

FIGURE 17.5 *Textured hair applied with liquid latex.*

Credit: Zeek Creative

Allow the adhesive time to dry before moving onto the next section.

EFFECT #2B: PATTERNING

The alternative to adding a three-dimensional object to the face is introducing a pattern into the makeup. Patterning is a great way to create demonic, draconic, or oceanic effects. They are relatively easy to achieve, but the effect can be dramatic especially when using different colors. Pattern colors work well with both cream makeup and powder makeup. Consider using iridescent eyeshadows to create ethereal effects.

- First, determine what type of pattern you would like for the character. Lace and fishnet tights are good fabrics to start with. Consider creating your own stencil on a lightweight, flexible surface – felt, foam, cloth, or paper – so it can be molded around the facial features.

- Second, lay the lace or stencil across the skin where the effect should be. Hold it steady with a hand or use low-tack masking tape to secure it in place.

- Finally, add the color with a sponge or brush. Blot or dab the color onto the skin through the lace or stencil. Using products with high pigment intensity is key. Blend several colors together to create three-dimensional effects. Remove the lace or stencil when finished with one section and repeat at different sections (see Figure 17.6).

FIGURE 17.6 *Patterning using cut hair net.*

Credit: Zeek Creative

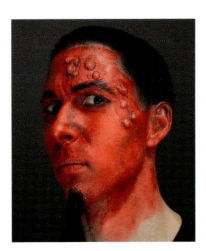

FIGURE 17.7 *Completed example of fantasy makeup 1.*

Credit: Zeek Creative

FIGURE 17.8 *Completed example of fantasy makeup 2.*

Credit: Zeek Creative

GLOSSARY

2" hair pin.   small pin used to secure a wig cap to pin-curls (used in wig styling)

3" hair pin (wig pin).   large hair pin used to secure light and medium weighted wigs to wig prep (used in wig styling)

5-prong comb.   a styling utensil with a comb on one end and a small five-prong pick at the other; the comb end has little ridges inside the tines which aid in back-combing (used for wig and hair styling)

additive color spectrum.   spectrum of light where the three primary colors – red, blue, green – combine to produce white light

artist color spectrum.   most commonly understood spectrum of color where the three primary colors are red, blue, and yellow. This spectrum only works with pigmented color and color products

bandage.   a length of medical bandage (used as a head wrap for short hair wig prep)

blemish.   any spot on the face or body that is red or pink in color

bobby pin.   small pin with two synching sides; one side is flat and the other is usually ridged (used to secure two hair sections together)

cake liner.   a water-based product that comes as a pressed powder and requires water to activate

ceruse.   a toxic mixture of white lead and vinegar, used during the Elizabethan period, to simulate a pale skin tone

chiaroscuro.   the process of using light and shadow to sculpt an object

color temperature.   a concept where each color relates to a different temperature – warm or cool. Most obvious warm colors include red, orange, and yellow; cool colors include blue, purple, and green

color theory.   relates to a set of color principles – how to make colors and how they react with other colors

complementary colors. colors located directly opposite each other on the color wheel and, when paired with their opposite, appear visually appealing

contamination transference. the concept where bacteria is transferred from one object to another and both become contaminated

corrective. a term of stage makeup that means to make facial features more symmetrical and is a basis for the basic makeup of a stage performer

dai. a blue mineral used by ancient Chinese cultures to color the eyebrows

duckbills. thin clamps that secure hair temporarily while styling

extrusion. wounds that tend to be isolated and enlarged such as boils or cysts

Geisha/Amazon pin. the largest sized hair pin, often 4 inches long (used to secure heavy wigs to wig prep)

hard-front wig. type of wig where the hairline is hard and straight across the forehead and are mostly machine-made

hue. synonym for color

intensity. a color at 100 percent saturation. Intensity can be low if the color is muted or it can be high when a color is its most brilliant or radiant

kohl. cosmetic developed in ancient Egypt to line the eye; made from burnt almonds, green malachite, lead, and manganese oxide

lace-front wig. type of wig with a piece of fine, mesh lace attached to the front of the wig.

Hair strands are tied into the mesh to simulate a natural hairline

local color. a color on a cloudless day with natural, sunlight radiating onto it

natural hair wigs. made from human hair or yak hair that have both a follicle and a root

Newton, Sir Isaac. (1642–1727) the first physicist to conduct experiments into the complexities of light. Using a prism, he discovered that pure light is comprised of seven colors – red, orange, yellow, green, cyan, indigo, and purple

over-drawing. a technique where the lipliner and lip color are taken past the natural lip shape

patching. the 18th century practice of using small pieces of fabric on the face as beauty marks and as a way to cover pox-marks

pop clips. small clips generally used in styling; clips snap together and are useful to secure the bandage to itself for a short hair wig prep

primary color. any of a set of three colors from which all other colors may be derived

pure hue. a mixed color that has one primary color at 100 percent intensity

rattail comb. a styling utensil with a comb on one end and a long thin point at the other end (used in styling wigs and hair)

secondary color. a color created when any two primary colors are mixed

shade. when black or darkness is added to a hue; the opposite of tint

spirit gum. most common theatrical adhesive used to attach prosthetic pieces and lace wigs to the skin

subtractive color spectrum.   spectrum of color that starts with the three secondary colors of the additive color spectrum – cyan, magenta, and yellow. This system works more with pigments than light where the three primary colors mix together to create black

synthetic hair.   plastic strands of hair that are smooth without a follicle and without a root; manufactured to look and move like natural hair

"T" pin.   a thin pin shaped like the letter "T" with a sharp, pointed end; not for use on human heads (used to secure wigs onto a canvas or Styrofoam wig block)

tertiary color.   a color created by mixing a primary color with its related secondary color

tint.   when white pigment or lightness is added to a hue; opposite of shade

tone.   when the pigment gray is added to the hue

toner.   product used to help rebalance the skin's natural pH level that is removed during washing

under-drawing.   the opposite of over-drawing where the lipliner and lip color are applied inside the natural lip shape

undertone.   the intrinsic, or underlying, color of an object

value.   the lightness or darkness of an object

ventilating.   the process of hand-tying hair strand-by-strand into wig lace

wig block.   a canvas stand to hold wigs when styling; usually made of canvas and filled with sawdust or cork (the best place to keep a styled wig during a production)

wig cap.   a nylon cap which covers pin-curls before a wig is applied

wig front.   the area where a wig meets the skin of the forehead

wig prep.   process of creating a flat, firm surface underneath a wig by utilizing pin-curls, wrapping the hair, and applying a wig cap

wigmaster.   the title of an individual who builds wigs, styles hair, and creates facial hair pieces for theatre, film, and opera

Young, Thomas.   (1773–1829) physicist who broadened Newton's experiments with light and deduced that only three of the seven light colors could produce white light – red, blue, and green. This spectrum is called the additive color spectrum

INDEX

References to figures are indicated in *italics*.